LUTHER

LUTHER

By ROBERT H. FISCHER

FRANK W. KLOS, Editor

GUSTAV REHBERGER, Illustrator

LUTHERAN CHURCH PRESS
PHILADELPHIA

LCA School of Religion Series

This pupil's book is accompanied by a teacher's guide,
Luther (SR 10, 11, 12).

3690K72 Printed in the United States of America   LB400

Who Is This Luther?

I ask that men call themselves not Lutherans but Christians. Who is this Luther? My teaching is not my own, nor have I been crucified for anyone. Why should it happen to me, miserable, stinking bag of worms that I am, that the children of Christ should be called by my insignificant name? I am not anybody's master, nor do I wish to be. With the one church I have in common the teaching of Christ who alone is our master.

—MARTIN LUTHER, 1522

Contents

PART ONE
Was This Reformation Necessary?

ERHALT UNS, HERR. L. M.

MARTIN LUTHER, 1483–1546
Based on Plainsong Melody, Mode H,
Jesu, dulcedo cordium

SECOND TUNE

Devotionally

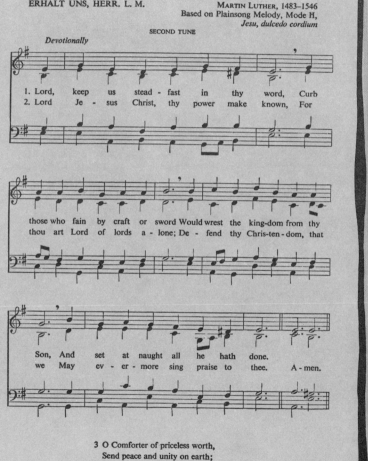

1. Lord, keep us stead - fast in thy word, Curb
2. Lord Je - sus Christ, thy power make known, For

those who fain by craft or sword Would wrest the king-dom from thy
thou art Lord of lords a - lone; De - fend thy Chris-ten - dom, that

Son, And set at naught all he hath done.
we May ev - er - more sing praise to thee. A - men.

3 O Comforter of priceless worth,
   Send peace and unity on earth;
   Support us in our final strife,
   And lead us out of death to life. Amen.

Martin Luther, 1483–1546
Tr. Catherine Winkworth, 1829–78

1. The Reformation: Greatness and Tragedy

He is a son of iniquity. He's a wild boar invading the Lord's vineyard. He split the seamless robe of Christ, the one holy church. He's a scabby sheep. He's a leper with a brain of brass and a nose of iron. He's a devil, a murderer, and corrupter of souls. He was fathered by a demon and his mother was a disreputable woman.

No! He is the German Hercules, who fights the many-headed dragon of the Roman church. He is the Saxon Huss, who had the courage to defy the church's tyranny. He is the Wittenberg nightingale, whose welcome song is the gospel of Christ. He is a second Apostle Paul.

Nonsense! He is a maniac. He is vulgar. He lacks all moderation. When the downtrodden peasants rose into action in response to his summons to freedom, he abandoned them and licked the boots of the princes. Windbag! Dr. Pussyfoot! Dr. Easychair! Pope of Wittenberg!

You're wrong! He is a dear man of God. He brought the gospel to light when it had been utterly lost. He is God's hero. He is the prophet of Germany. He is the Elijah of these last days.

With such words people took sides over Martin Luther in his own day. People still take sides today: He was a depraved, dissolute man. No, he revived the morals of Europe. He was the champion of the free conscience. No, he chained consciences with his rigid dogmas. He was a profound thinker. No, he had a poor education and an erratic mind. With his advice that men must always obey the state, he became the ancestor of Hitler. Nonsense! It was Luther who inspired the heroic Norwegian resistance to Hitler.

How can we account for this strong compulsion that people feel to take a stand for or against Martin Luther? Whether they know much or little about him, they still have an opinion. How many other historical characters can you name who continue, century after century, not only to fascinate scholars, but also to arouse the simplest people to take sides?

A Man and His Course

At first glance the remarkable thing is not that Luther became as famous as he did, but that he achieved any fame at all. The odds

11

were against it. In the partly restless, partly sleepy, overripe feudal age of five hundred years ago, the only persons likely to attain more than local fame, even during their lifetime, were great nobles and warriors and church dignitaries—and a few adventurers and princes of culture. Luther was no such man of the world. He came from peasant stock. He became a monk and a priest at a time when ridicule for such callings seemed almost as common as respect. The only eminent position that he held was that of Bible professor in a puny school trying to become a respectable university. In this position he remained for over thirty-three years, until his death. He had no ambition to become a public reformer. God had led him along, he said, like a horse with blinders on.

The main point, however, is that he did follow a particular course, and he held faithfully to it. Because of his life and work, the Western world has been radically changed. Because of his career, whenever Christians today try to understand how the church came to be what it is, they examine Luther's insights for one important clue to the answer. Because of his career, whenever a Christian asks himself what he is doing with his own life, Luther's life furnishes a remarkable mirror. His life shows us how one great Christian faced the challenges of his day and tried to meet them as a responsible Christian in the presence of God. Luther was far from infallible, not always successful, not always wise. But he did try to be faithful. This, after all, is the way most truly great men become great. They see more clearly than others what the deepest problems of their day are, and then they work away at them more forcefully and persistently than others.

The great problems to which Luther addressed himself will unfold before us as we proceed. Luther exercised an influence, not only upon religion, but also upon the common life of home and daily work, upon politics, social relations, and education. He left his imprint on music and literature and even on everyday language. But all this was simply the by-product of his concern over deeper and more intimate problems: how a man stands with God, what a man's character and action should be in the sight of God. These are basic problems, and once a person has raised them, he cannot escape them. It was this concern over life in the presence of God that gave Luther a sense of direction as he responded to practical and public problems. No wonder, then, that in all sorts of matters men had to take notice of Luther's thought. The things he spoke and wrote about penetrated to the depths of man's personal life. He helped them bring their most pressing concerns to a conscious level.

Fascinating as Martin Luther is, however, we cannot concern ourselves with him merely as an individual. We cannot understand his life apart from the church to which he devoted his life.

The State of the Church

The church in Luther's day needed a drastic reform. Candid Roman Catholics today admit this as readily as do Protestants. But did the church need a reform that would split it into fragments? Luther's admirers portrayed him as a Hercules cleansing the filthy Augean stables—the church. Others felt he did not cleanse the stables; he wrecked them.

Many sincere Christians believed that the necessary reforms could be effected within the existing structure of the church. One such person was Sebastian Brant, doctor of laws and literary adviser to printers in Basel, who wrote the famous allegorical poem *The Ship of Fools* when Luther was eleven years old. Brant believed that the Roman Catholic church was Christ's own body and needed only to be administered purely. He died in 1521, firmly opposed to the upstart Luther. Erasmus, prince of the northern humanists, also criticized the church bitingly and yearned for a thorough reformation. But he wanted it to be a peaceful one. He was accused of laying the egg that Luther hatched. "No," retorted Erasmus, "the egg I laid became a gentle hen; Luther hatched a fighting cock!" Erasmus, like Brant, kept his peace with Rome. So did Dr. Staupitz, Luther's beloved monastic superior from whom he received so much help on his way to understanding the gospel. To these and many other persons, Luther's movement constituted disobedience to, if not outright rebellion against, Christ and his church.

Undeniably, a splintering took place. But in what sense was it a splitting of the church? The answer to this question is not simple. Is the church of Christ identical with the Roman Catholic church? If so, the Protestants split off from the church, "founded churches," and caused numerous schisms. But neither Luther nor his fellow Protestant reformers would accept this explanation. All of them intended not to innovate but to renovate—to restore the one true church to the pattern Christ had intended, to liberate the church from the "captivity" in which Roman Catholicism had kept it.

Laudable as the ideals and intentions of all the reformers were, however, there were many splits among the people of Christ. Actually, the Reformation was not a single movement; it was a number of varied religious reform programs, including a reform within the Roman Catholic church. There were as many different programs

13

as there were views of what was really wrong with the church and what was needed to correct it.

The fearful cost of these splits for the church is virtually unmeasurable. Out of the splits came widespread mistrust and even hatred of Christians for one another. Out of the splits came bitter wars and persecutions. Out of the splits came efforts by each group to build up its fences to keep Christ and his gospel "inside"—fences of theological formulas or patterns of worship or forms of organization or codes of morality. Yet all too often the fences kept out those whom Christ came into the world to seek—perhaps at times kept Christ himself out. All of these groups betrayed one-sidedness in contrast to the fullness of Christ. Worse still, they all betrayed lovelessness. Each "church" tended to pursue its own advantage in rivalry with the others, and all too often this stood in the way of its proclamation of Christ's message to the world.

No church body is exempt from this judgment. To what extent, then, is the Reformation itself to blame? Some observers, for example, see in Protestantism the very principle of divisiveness—each group for itself, every man for himself—and they see Luther as the man who started it all. On the other hand it can be maintained that in a real sense the Reformation—Protestant and Catholic together—reversed the trend of religious decay and made the Christian faith an urgent concern once more. It can hardly be said that the gospel came to hold free sway in European life, but at least the gospel had a new chance, for men began to ask with renewed concern exactly what the gospel is and what allegiance they owe it. The price of that renewed questioning was the dividedness of their varying answers.

Effects on the World

The importance of the Reformation does not lie only in its effects upon the Christian church. The church lives not for itself, but to be a light in the world. We must therefore examine the effects of the Reformation upon the world at large.

One can make a good case for the fact that Protestantism helped us gain our modern freedoms and speeded our social and economic progress. Has it not contributed to the liberation of the human spirit and to a larger understanding of man's rights and responsibilities in the common life? For example, Roman Catholicism had declared that its teachings on beliefs and morals had no less than divine authority. It therefore claimed the right to impose its will upon government and upon society and the right to stifle any idea of which it disapproved. Half a century after the Reformation began, the pope declared Queen Elizabeth's subjects released from allegiance to her because she was not an obedient Catholic, and he invited other monarchs to invade England with his blessing. Even a century after Luther's time, the Roman Catholic church forced the scientist Galileo to deny his conviction that the earth revolves around the sun. Part of Luther's program was to tear down this tyrannous, idolatrous claim, this "wall" with which the Roman Catholic church prevented any effective reform. Underlying that program was his insistence that no man or group of men is infallible, even in the church.

On the other hand, a case can be made for the idea that the Protestant Reformation bears responsibility for modern worldliness. Didn't Protestantism cut men adrift from the authority of the church which had produced a "unified Christian society?" Does Protestantism, then, eventually tend to turn men's minds from a religious outlook on life to an exclusive interest in earthly happiness, from the pursuit of truth to the pursuit of personal advantage?

To understand and evaluate the Reformation, we must first turn to Martin Luther. But the Reformation is no one-man story. Luther did not simply start the Reformation out of nothing; many leaders before him had yearned for a reform of church and society. Nor did he force a revolt upon unwilling people. He could not have gained such an immediate and widespread response if many people had not already felt that things were deeply wrong with the old system. But Luther is the man who actually set the Protestant Reformation in motion. By examining both the man and his career, we shall be led close to the heart of the Reformation in all its greatness and its tragedy. To understand Luther properly, however, we must first know what European life was like on the eve of the Reformation.

2. Life at the Eve of the Reformation

WHAT could a gifted boy expect of life in Europe long ago? How should he plan his career? The answer varied, depending upon when he lived and where.

Social Conditions

About A.D. 1000 when feudalism held sway, the answer would depend largely on how you were born: noble or serf. Nobles owned estates. Serfs, although not personal slaves, belonged with the land. If you were born a serf, you remained a serf on the land where you were born. The only exception to this fixed social system was the church. It was the one institution in which a person could rise according to his personal ability, in the priesthood or in a monastic order. But since advancement usually required at least modest education, it was uncommon for a member of the lower class to qualify.

Five hundred years later, when Martin Luther was a youth, the situation had changed considerably. There was a much wider range of choice for a career. The fixed social order where every person knew his place in life—his rights and his duties—was crumbling, although at different rates of speed in different places. At about the time of the Crusades (roughly 1095–1450), and in considerable measure because of their influence, an urban society based on commerce began to arise alongside the feudal order based on land. The Crusades had stimulated a desire for new commodities, new freedoms, and new adventures. By doing this, the Crusades had dislocated the labor market. So had the Black Plague, appearing about 1347.

In many areas, therefore, since laborers were in such great demand, serfs had become free peasants, either tenant farmers or paid workers. Both peasants and younger sons of the nobility increasingly sought their fortunes in the towns. Starting with nothing, a young man might enter a trade and rise to respectability as an artisan. Another, like Luther's father, Hans, leasing a few smelting furnaces, might attain a modest living and local prestige. For his son he could have higher ambitions: to study law and then enter the service of a nobleman or a town council, and perhaps marry the daughter of a well-to-do citizen. With rare luck one might even rise to fantastic wealth and influence, like Dick Whittington, three times lord mayor of London, or Jacques Coeur, the French financial baron who was so wealthy that he could lend the king of France enough money to fight a war. At the other extreme, of course, there were others—countless others—who lived and died in the grinding poverty of the spreading urban slums, far worse off than the rural peasants.

All this meant that by Luther's day the social structure, once neatly fixed, had become mobile and sprawling. Once society had consisted of three classes—serfs, nobles, and churchmen. Now in addition to the churchmen, nobles, and some serfs, there were also rural peasants, town proletarians, petty artisans, upper-class artisans who controlled monopolistic guilds (organizations of craftsmen, such as weavers, tailors, smiths, bakers), and financial magnates—bankers and investment adventurers. The latter, with their vast enterprises and their loans at twelve to fifty percent interest, often rivaled in wealth the landed nobles, who were caught between fixed income and rising prices. No wonder there was widespread social unrest.

Rise of Nationalism

A youth's expectations in Luther's day also depended on which part of Europe he lived in. In the heyday of western European social unity, about 1200–1250, there was theoretically one supreme political power, the Holy Roman Empire; one church, obedient to the pope; and one language, Latin, understood by educated men from Sweden to Portugal, from Scotland to Sicily. But this "one Christian society" proved unstable. Indeed, the papacy's impressive power in the thirteenth century was bought at the price of clipping the empire's wings and encouraging nationalism. Once nationalism began to grow, it could not be stopped. By about 1340 France and England, the first two "nations" in anything like the modern sense, had developed enough energy and ambition to launch a long, on-and-off struggle, called the Hundred Years' War, for possession of the territory of Aquitaine. Joan of Arc took part in it, as did Edward the Black Prince and a succession of famous English kings—Richard II, Henry IV, and Henry V.

There were no other centralized powers in Europe until Ferdinand and Isabella, Columbus' patrons, brought feudal Spain like a meteor into the forefront of international politics. Germany was still a patchwork of tiny principalities, mostly backward and brawling, and a number of free cities. Italy was disunited, too, and the popes hoped to keep it that way.

But national ambitions were alive everywhere. In the late Middle Ages, literature began to be written, not just in Latin, but in many languages, including Italian and German, and national pride showed itself in the mutual hatred of Englishmen and Frenchmen, Germans and Italians. France and England simply ignored the "Empire," which more and more became in essence a matter of German politics. Indeed, with the growing national rivalries, the Holy Roman Empire was in danger of becoming an empty ideal. At one time, not too long before Luther, the emperors even hired their troops out to kings as mercenary soldiers. Then for one brief period the empire again became a mighty force before sinking into final obscurity. That was when it passed into the hands of Charles V, who swore never to come to terms with the German heretic, Martin Luther.

Power politics, however, is sometimes surprising. Mighty church and mighty empire declared Luther a dangerous heretic and outlaw.

Yet throughout his lifetime, church and empire were unable to squelch his reformation, because of a three-way rivalry among the "Holy Roman" emperor and the "Most Christian" king of France and "His Holiness" the pope.

The Renaissance

Another movement was profoundly changing the patterns of life in some parts of western Europe during the youth of Hans Luther and that of his son. The Renaissance, which means "rebirth," was reaching its height in Italy about 1450 and for three generations thereafter. Fictional accounts and even histories of the Renaissance are often too lurid, too gory, too romanticized. It is even an exaggeration to depict it, in contrast to the Middle Ages, as an altogether new "discovery of the world and of man." Without doubt, however, a different temper and outlook on life were gradually emerging. More and more, men devoted themselves to life in this world. More and more eagerly they pursued the goals of self-fulfillment and individual freedom. The tendency grew to make man (even oneself, personally) the "measure of all things." Ancient Greek and Roman culture, rediscovered at that time, provided an exciting model for the cultivation of art and literature and exciting ideas as to how life should be lived. The elite artists and authors of the Renaissance might be patronized by churchmen or might even be churchmen themselves, but the net effect of this movement was to undercut or bypass the religious view of life which had served as the model of medieval Christian society. But the spread of the movement was neither sudden nor complete. Moreover the type of Renaissance which gained a foothold in France and England and Germany —but not until Luther's boyhood—displayed in general a more sober and conservative frame of mind than the Italian type.

By Luther's day, at any rate, European culture was becoming a churning sea of conflicting attitudes toward thought and morals and life in general. The invention of printing, one generation before Luther's birth, gave an enormous impetus to the spread of ideas, comparable only to the twentieth century's gifts of radio and television, and a corresponding impetus to popular education, comparable to today's vast literacy campaigns in the far corners of the earth.

Discovery and Turmoil

This, too, was the age of discovery. Beginning about 1450, maritime exploration quickly developed into a scramble for land and riches. For young men in some parts of Europe, here was an exciting

18

answer to the question of planning careers. Spain reaped the initial advantage: Columbus set sail westward when Luther was a boy of nine, and Magellan launched his voyage to circle the globe the year Luther disputed with John Eck over the power of the pope. England, France, and Holland made their challenges later. Germany never entered the contest until late in the nineteenth century.

Neither Renaissance ideas nor exploration fever shaped Luther's youth. Few German boys of his day were ambitious to paint great pictures or write literary masterpieces. Fewer still were inflamed by tales of adventuresome voyages, sea monsters, and distant, wealthy lands. Life in the petty feudal states of Thuringia and Saxony was much more confined and conservative. Far more exciting to Saxons were grandfatherly stories of raids by Hussite heretics from Bohemia across the border and current news of the advance of the fearsome Turks, who had taken Constantinople in 1453 and were destined, in 1529, to besiege Vienna, only four hundred miles away. Would the infidels engulf Christian Europe as they had nearly done eight hundred years before? The scholar Sebastian Brant feared they might. With little exaggeration he wrote that they controlled the Mediterranean, and "the Danube too is now their own."

The Turkish tide was advancing. Germans had to forge some kind of unity to resist it. The emperor wanted to call a crusade against the Turks. An Austrian or Hungarian or Bavarian or Saxon boy would be wise to ponder the need for military leaders in the coming international crisis if he wanted to plan his career ambitiously.

3. The Church

ALTHOUGH exploration and crusading had a fine ring to them, more should go into the planning of a life than the ambition for fame and riches, more even than the desire to be a useful citizen. Everywhere the church reminded men that they have not only an earthly body but also an eternal soul. They should be "in the world but not of the world," for this transitory life is merely a pilgrimage toward glorious heaven—or toward endless, flaming hell. Men should lay up treasures in heaven rather than on earth. Best-selling books in the infancy of printing bore such titles as *The Imitation of Christ, Contempt of the World, On the Art of Dying.*

The Church's Influence

There were people who ignored the church's teaching, of course. But we today find it hard to realize how very far the church's influence reached in the Middle Ages. The church was still generally regarded as the "ark of salvation" bearing the faithful safely through the storms of life to the haven of heaven. "Outside of the church there is no salvation." Its status in society was fixed by law. The Christian religion alone was entitled to full legal protection, for error has no equal rights with truth. What the church decreed in any religious case, the civil government was bound to enforce. This was the way laws developed for nearly a thousand years. For example, anyone who denied the doctrine of the Trinity or rebaptized a person was subject to death.

The church of Rome, of course, was the true church, said western Europe, though Greek-speaking Christendom in the east scorned the claim. The church of Rome, indeed, had shown impressive effectiveness. During the Middle Ages it had launched a project of breathtaking boldness: It would actualize on earth Augustine's ideal of the "City of God," the community ruled by God. With patience, sometimes with crudity, but also with genuine Christian holiness, the church had converted and civilized the barbarians and had directed the upbuilding of the medieval Christian society. It owned perhaps a third to half of the land in western Europe. It generally controlled education. It claimed superiority over all civil governments: "As much as the soul is worthier than the body, so much worthier is the priesthood than the monarchy." Of this priesthood the pope was the head. "No king can rule rightly unless he devoutly serves Christ's vicar." In Peter's and in his successors' hands, said Pope Boniface VIII in 1302, "are the two swords, spiritual and temporal. Both are in the power of the church. The latter is to be used on behalf of the church, the former by the church. The temporal power ought to be subject to the spiritual power. Therefore it is altogether necessary for salvation for every human creature to be subject to the Roman pope."

The church not only influenced the great affairs of society; it also reached into and enveloped the daily existence of the common man. Wherever he walked, churches, monasteries, and a thousand wayside crosses loomed to remind him of the seriousness of life and the greatness of the church's authority. Whenever he listened, the church taught him how to live a good life and merit salvation. Even if he did not listen, the church had powers of discipline in private and public morals. Sinful mankind could not achieve a good life without divine grace. As the custodian of grace, the church administered it through seven sacraments which covered all the major events and needs of life from the cradle to the grave. Corresponding to man's earthly birth, growth, daily food, daily washing, and preparation for death were the Sacraments of Baptism, Confirmation, Holy Communion, Penance, and Extreme Unction, while the Sacraments of Marriage and Holy Orders provided for the proper continuance of the human race and of the church's priesthood.

Every activity of life required divine blessing and protection from the superhuman powers of evil—the closing of a business deal, the safety of a journey, the care of crops and livestock, the cure of illness. The church had a concern for men's souls and for their bodies. It said Masses and prayed for the souls of the living on earth and the dead in purgatory. It supervised the care of the sick and the relief of the poor. It directly affected the working man's calendar: For every three or four working days there was a holiday (literally, a holy day) to be observed with religious acts or just plain time off.

Either ambition for a career or zeal to serve God and man, therefore, might move a medieval boy to enter the holy priesthood or a monastic order.

Loss of Prestige

By Luther's day, however, the church's power had been pared down and the church's prestige badly battered. Gone was the time when a Pope Gregory VII could keep the emperor waiting barefoot in the snow to beg forgiveness. No longer could a pope induce the mightiest monarchs of Christendom to forsake their fortunes and responsibilities at home in order—at their own expense—to launch a crusade to the Holy Land. The days were past when a Pope Innocent III could successfully depose an emperor, force a proud king of France to take back a dismissed wife, or receive the entire kingdom of Englands as his feudal possession from a king under church discipline. Innocent reigned in the early thirteenth century; less than a hundred years later the kings of France dictated papal elections and kept the popes under their thumb at the town of Avignon. After seventy years of this scandalous "captivity" of the church, a new pope determined to return to Rome. But when he did so, a group of cardinals elected another pope who would remain at Avignon.

Now what would you do if it was "altogether necessary for salvation" to be obedient to the bishop of Rome? To be on the safe side, an ordinary person might follow his ruler. But while the kings of England and Naples recognized the pope at Rome as the rightful pope, the kings of France and Scotland obeyed the one at Avignon. "Oh, but this is a spiritual matter: Let us consult the leading churchmen." But the cardinals and bishops were divided. So were the theologians at the universities. "Then let us ask the living saints, persons with a reputation of holiness." But the holy Catherine of Siena insisted that the pope of Rome was the true vicar of Christ, while the holy Vincent Ferrer damned the Roman pope's supporters and insisted that the pope at Avignon held the keys of Peter. Not until 1417, after forty years of this scandal, was the Great Western Schism healed, and before that happened there were even three popes at once. The average citizen was hopelessly confused.

No wonder the prestige of the papacy sagged sickeningly. Critics sharply challenged the church's claim of supremacy over civil government and the pope's supremacy over the church. Resentment became bitter, especially in England and Germany, against demands for money to support papal wars or magnificent building programs in Avignon or Rome. Prophets predicted woes. The saying went around that since the beginning of the Great Schism, no souls had been admitted to heaven.

With the slogan, "A reform of the church in head and members!" the Council of Constance finally healed the schism and designed a plan to remove many abuses in the church. But two great ironies attach to this church council. In the first place its leaders, sincere reformers, decreed the burning of another sincere reformer, John Huss. Second, the council set forth the bold claim that not the pope, but the representative assembly of bishops is the final authority in the church. This would make church government a parliamentary monarchy instead of an absolute monarchy. The new pope objected. The council retorted that if its power were not superior, it could not have eliminated the three rival popes, and therefore his election would not be valid. Nevertheless, within thirty years the conciliar movement collapsed in confusion and the papacy was once more in firm control.

The church's unity now seemed secure, but the church's health continued to decline. There were still some spiritually earnest groups, but the piety of the people by and large was woefully superficial. People attended Mass and heard it in Latin, which they could not understand. They received little instruction and little preaching of the Word of God. Their religious activities were overloaded with the mechanical performance of "good works," such as pilgrimages, processions, and the purchase of indulgences, to get rid of their sins. The monastic orders, once the vanguard of the church's constructive program, were generally in disrepute. Theology at the universities had degenerated into hairsplitting.

Open Corruption

The most obvious of all symptoms of the church's illness was the corruption of the "Renaissance papacy" which ruled from about 1450 until well after the Reformation broke out. Popes shamelessly sold church offices, promoted the public careers of their children, conducted wars to enlarge their territories, and reveled in luxury and artistic splendor. Many of the cardinals and bishops imitated the popes as best they could. It is ironic to think, as one looks at the awe-inspiring church of St. Peter in Rome: This church played a role in starting the Protestant Reformation. St. Peter's was being built with proceeds from the very indulgences that touched off Luther's explosion.

In 1514 a play by Erasmus was produced in Paris entitled *Julius Excluded*. In it Julius II, the warrior pope and planner of St. Peter's who had died a year before, demands entrance at the gate of heaven, boldly boasting of the glories he has brought to Rome and blandly admitting his chicanery in office and his vices in private life. The amazed apostle Peter asks if there is no way to remove a wicked pope. No, replies Julius, only a council can correct a pope, and a council has to have the pope's approval. Can he not be removed for any crime? Every time the dismayed Peter mentions one, Julius blithely tops him with a worse one which cannot be punished:

JULIUS: Some say there is one cause for which a pope can be deposed.

PETER: When he has done something good, I suppose, since he is not to be punished for his bad deeds!

JULIUS: If he can be publicly convicted of heresy. But this is impossible, too. For he can cancel any canon he does not like. Or he can recant.

PETER: Fortunate pope, who can cheat Christ with his laws! Quite true, the remedy in such a case is not in a council.

The satirical author was more of a prophet than he knew. Three years later, Luther's Ninety-Five Theses set off the chain of events that resulted in a painful and tragic remedy. Biting literary satire and lampooning woodcuts could be laughed off. Annoying reformers could be declared heretics and outlawed or burned. One might have expected that the church would take warning when, at

23

frequent intervals from about 1450 on, the diet (parliament) of the empire solemnly drew up lists of serious "grievances" regarding religious conditions in Germany—Rome's financial extortion, churchmen's gross negligence and immorality. But nothing happened.

Signs of Life

It would be wrong, however, to think that Christianity was utterly dead. A striking tale by the fourteenth century Italian storyteller Boccaccio sets the religious picture in a different light. Jack (Jaennot), a silk merchant in Paris, urges his fellow merchant Abraham to accept the Christian faith. Finally Abraham says, "I shall go to Rome and take a look at the pope and his cardinals. If their lives convince me that your religion is better than mine, I shall become a Christian." Jack tries desperately to dissuade Abraham. But he fails. Eventually Abraham returns from Rome. With scant hope Jack seeks him out. "I saw neither holiness nor devotion nor anything good in the clergy of Rome," begins Abraham, "but the very opposite, luxury, greed, gluttony, and still worse things. The court of Rome seems more a forge of the devil's work than of things divine. For all I see, the pope and the rest are working with all their might to destroy the Christian religion." Jack's heart sinks into his shoes. But Abraham continues, "And yet, in spite of their efforts, your religion is gaining in strength and glory every day! Plainly it is upheld by the Spirit of God. I want to become a Christian. Please go with me to the church and have me baptized into your holy faith."

Boccaccio, no special friend of the church, had merely set out to write a clever and entertaining story. But out of it emerged a remarkable testimony that even when churchmen are unholy, the church of Jesus Christ remains holy.

The Christian faith was alive, all right. From his peasant mother, the boy Luther learned the Lord's Prayer and the Ave Maria, the Ten Commandments and the creed, just as the peasant maid Joan of Arc and thousands of others did. Sincere laymen banded together in the Order of the Brothers of the Common Life to cultivate prayer and Bible reading and to support schools and serve the needy. Sincere priests tried to restore seriousness and faithfulness among the clergy, in the monasteries, in public life. Christian humanists called for an expansion of education to train leaders with a conscience devoted to purifying church and state, and to spread the "craft of Christian living"—the simple imitation of Jesus.

But just as undeniably, the prevailing mood was pessimism and uneasiness. The age seemed overripe and decaying. Reform measures seemed piecemeal, partial, temporary, powerless to effect a genuine renewal. Somehow they did not strike to the source of the decay, did not set forth a great program around which men would rally. Even so faithful a champion of the old order as Sebastian Brant was convinced that the church was not "gaining in strength and glory every day," but was ebbing and receding.

> St. Peter's ship is tossed around,
> I greatly fear it may go down.
> I'm tempted candidly to say:
> We do approach the Judgment Day.
> Since mercy's held in cold despite,
> We're now approaching total night.
> Though such things have not happened yet,
> The vessel sways—it may upset!

PART TWO
Luther's Way to the Gospel

VOM HIMMEL HOCH. L. M.   MARTIN LUTHER, 1483–1546

In flowing style

1. From heaven a - bove to earth I come To
2. To you this night is born a child Of

bear good news to ev - ery home; Glad ti - dings of
Ma - ry, cho - sen moth - er mild; This lit - tle child,

great joy I bring, Where - of I now will say and sing.
of low - ly birth, Shall be the joy of all the earth.

3 Were earth a thousand times as fair,
Beset with gold and jewels rare,
She yet were far too poor to be
A narrow cradle, Lord, to thee.

4 Ah, dearest Jesus, Holy Child,
Make thee a bed, soft undefiled,
Within my heart, that it may be
A quiet chamber kept for thee.

5 'Glory to God in highest heaven,
Who unto man his Son hath given,'
While angels sing with pious mirth
A glad new year to all the earth.

Martin Luther, 1483–1546
Tr. Catherine Winkworth, 1829–78

4. The Vow in the Storm

So packed with drama was the entire career of Martin Luther that we run the danger of becoming utterly confused as one colorful event follows another. So much material has been written about him that no one can digest it all. In addition, both friends and enemies have confused the picture with half-truths, untruths, and partisan, uncritical emotions.

Like Abraham Lincoln, Luther belongs not to the historians but to the mass of people, important though the historian is for insuring the accuracy of the portrait. The basic lines of Luther's life and message are accessible to all of us. Luther spoke the language of ordinary people, through sermons, popular tracts, hymns, liturgies, and catechisms, through his translation of the Bible, and through his personal leadership. The people responded, and the face of Christendom was changed. Though today's world is vastly different, Luther still holds an astonishing power to move men's hearts and minds. His personality still retains its color and vitality; his teachings nourish and stimulate simple believers as well as profound scholars. Much of his thinking is amazingly contemporary.

Our story will therefore concentrate upon the Luther who shared the struggles that you and I must face in the presence of God, the Luther whose life work belonged to the people of God, the Luther who can guide us in our modern complex living.

Let us look first at what turned the promising law student into a monk, and what turned the young monk, preoccupied with the salvation of his soul, into a blazing reformer who "lifted a world off its hinges and shaped something new."

A Fateful Decision

For more than twenty years the famous Dr. Luther had students boarding at his house in Wittenberg. Eagerly, if not always accurately, they filled notebooks with the remarks they heard at mealtime. After his death, his students collected these remarks into a large and lovely volume titled *Table Talk*. One such notebook entry takes us into Luther's dining room on July 16, 1539. We hear the doctor saying (if the reporter recorded it correctly), "Today we are at the time of year when I entered the monastery at Erfurt." The student

27

noted further, "And he began to recite the story how he had made his vow. Two weeks earlier, on the road near Stotternheim, not far from Erfurt, he was thrown into such a panic by a bolt of lightning that he cried out in terror, 'Help, St. Anne, I will become a monk!' 'Afterward I regretted my vow, and many tried to change my mind. But I was determined to go through with it, and on the evening of the 16th I held a farewell party for some good friends, whom I wanted to conduct me to the monastery on the morrow.' They tried to hold him back, but he said, 'Today you see me for the last time, and then no more!' 'Then they accompanied me, with tears in their eyes. My father was very angry over my vow, but I held to my purpose. I never considered leaving the monastery. I had become purely dead to the world . . .' "

Our scrap of *Table Talk* offers us an excellent base of operations for exploring Luther's youth. In the first place, it forces us to ask how accurate our sources of information are. Already the clumsy style of the reporter makes us wonder if he is reliable; perhaps he colored the story. An astounding number of legends about Luther did arise in just that fashion. Furthermore can we trust the memory of the elderly, talkative, cranky Dr. Luther as he tries to recall an event that happened over a third of a century before?

Other Accounts

Let us examine two more samples of the story of Luther's vow. In 1521, while he was cooped up in the Wartburg Castle, Luther wrote a lengthy treatise on monasticism. In a moving, affectionate dedication to his father he says, "I remember only too clearly that when you had calmed down and were talking with me, I declared that I had been called by terrors from heaven; for not willingly and eagerly did I become a monk, much less to gratify my belly, but walled around with the terror and agony of sudden death, I vowed a forced and necessary vow."

This statement which Luther wrote only sixteen years after the event does not specifically mention the lightning bolt. And a still earlier account exists. In 1519, just as Luther's trouble with the Roman Catholic church was approaching the explosion point, Crotus Rubeanus, a former fellow student at Erfurt and now a famous scholar, wrote Luther a letter of encouragement. "Go on, as you have begun! Leave an example to the future. You do this not without inspiration of the gods. Divine Providence intended this when, as you were returning from your parents, a stroke of lightning from heaven flung you to the ground like another Paul before the town of Erfurt and, to our deep distress, forced your departure from our company into the Augustinian walls."

These three major accounts actually harmonize rather well, though small differences are apparent. Discrepancies in records are a problem that haunts any attempt to establish facts. We must beware believing everything we find in any record, and we must doubly beware of imaginative attempts to pad the story. But now that this problem has been pointed out, we may proceed. After all, it is not the records which absorb our interest, but the man whom the records reveal.

The story of the Stotternheim vow presents an interesting picture of the young Luther. His vow seems odd. Was it simply the cry of an oversensitive and terrified youth, or was it a wild promise of an eccentric, emotionally unbalanced person? In any case we find it strange today that in such a crisis Luther should think of entering a monastery. Perhaps some deep rebellion within him is erupting. Rebellion against what? An unhappy background of poverty? A harsh home? Poor schooling? Several records emphasize that Luther's father was furious at his son's vow. What was Luther's relationship with his parents?

5. Luther at Home

A son was born to Hans and Margaret Luther in their modest cottage at Eisleben, Thuringia, on November 10, 1483. Very properly, his parents had him baptized at the parish church on the following day, naming him Martin after the saint whose martyrdom was celebrated on the eleventh.

Short, heavyset Hans Luther was an ambitious man. Coming from a long line of Saxon peasant farmers, he had gone into copper mining with the hope of rising in the world, first in Eisleben and then, when Martin was six months old, in nearby Mansfeld. Martin later remarked, "My father, as a young man, was a poor miner. My mother gathered firewood in the forest and carried home on her back all that was needed in the house. The harsh conditions forced them to work hard." This picture of family poverty must not be exaggerated, however. For a wife to gather firewood was not at all unusual. Soon, in any case, through hard work and thrift, the family fortune began to rise. By about the time Martin started school, his father was elected by the commoners as their representative to the town council, an indication of his economic independence and of the respect of the townsmen. Eventually prosperous enough to lease and manage several copper mines, Hans could dream of still better things for his eldest son.

For a German just working his way up socially toward a village middle class, this dream would take a perfectly definite form. Two dignified professions were within reach of his son: law and the church. The latter alternative Hans scorned, God-fearing though he was. Like many of his class, he did not consider the monastic life very desirable, and he regarded the great swarm of priests with very little esteem. Besides, how would a priest be able to care for his parents in their old age or continue the ancestral name with a family of his own? No, law was the profession for his son. Martin might make a name as a public official or lawyer in some Saxon town, or with luck achieve a position in the court of Duke Frederick. He might win the hand of a young woman from a reputable family. "You planned for me a respectable and wealthy marriage," wrote Martin later in a reminiscent mood.

If the goal seemed clear, so did the path. Hans' son should be trained to upright character, hard work, and piety, and be given the best education his father could afford. Training in character, work, and piety began at home. As everyone knew, character begins with learning what is right, and learning what is right begins with obedience to parents and other persons in authority. The Middle Ages took the ancient proverb seriously: "He who spares the rod hates his son, but he who loves him is diligent to discipline him" (Proverbs 13:24). Like most children, Martin long remembered his parents' diligence. "My father once whipped me so that I ran away from him and felt ugly toward him until he took pains to win me back." "Once my mother whipped me till the blood came, for taking a nut. Such strict discipline drove me to the monastery, though she meant well." He remarked that circumstances were not always taken into account, and severity sometimes outran fairness.

But these recollections do not show a boy estranged from his parents. The general atmosphere of the home may have been more somber than gay, but good cheer and care and kindness were evident, too. Martin's single remark connecting discipline with his vow to enter the monastery should not be overemphasized. Indeed, even when he made the above statements, Martin recalled that his father took pains to win him back, and that his mother meant well when she whipped him. Deep respect and affection are unmistakable in Luther's dealings with his parents in later life, at any rate. In the

30

dedication letter accompanying his treatise on monastic vows, he wrote of Hans' fatherly love, closing with these tender words, "The Lord bless you, my dear father, and my mother—your pearl—and our whole family." When Hans was suffering his last illness, Martin wrote to ask if he could be brought to Wittenberg. "I would be most happy if you and mother could come here, and my wife Katie and all of us beg with tears that you will do so. It would be a heartfelt joy to me to be with you again, and show my gratitude to God and to you according to the fourth commandment, with the devotion and service of a good son."

Perhaps the best proof of Luther's abiding respect for his parents' care is his teaching on this very commandment. Sturdy Hans Luther had flung the words at him bitterly when Martin went into the monastery and the priesthood, "Have you never read, 'Honor your father and your mother'?" The words stuck in his heart. What Martin had been taught as a boy, he taught as a man. In his *Large Catechism,* Luther eloquently insisted that honor to parents is the very foundation of all human authority. "Young people must be taught to revere their parents as representatives of God, and to remember that however lowly, poor, feeble, and queer they may be, they are their own father and mother, given them by God." Obedience to them "is the greatest work that we can do, next to the sublime worship of God," and the proper expression of "gratitude for the kindness and all the good things we have received from our parents." For Luther, there was no other way to live.

Clearly, character-building and religion belonged together for Hans and Margaret Luther. They were God-fearing people. They might have a low regard for priests, but they were faithful in attending Mass, and they prayed at their son's bedside. They accepted the Church's teaching that men's duty was to maintain the proper balance between hope and fear before God: hope that they had his grace and had done enough to please him, fear that they may have lost his grace or may not have done enough. Meanwhile, to be on the safe side, they also did their best not to run afoul of all the spirits that lurked everywhere. The peasantry was sure that evil spirits stole eggs and butter or turned milk sour. Devils caused misfortune, sickness, insanity, and death; witches could summon them. Margaret Luther in particular was firmly convinced of these things, and even Martin never worked himself free of them. "In my native country," he once remarked at table, "on top of a high mountain called the Pubelsberg is a lake. If a stone is thrown into it, a storm will arise over the whole region, because the waters are the abode of captive demons." Actually it was not only the uneducated who were concerned over demons and witches. When Martin was a child, a learned churchman had written a long book on witches and how to deal with them. Later, Luther and his fellow pastors had to handle many cases involving devils and witches; his friend, Pastor Bugenhagen, was considered especially skillful in thwarting them.

6. Luther at School

WHAT do you know of the rod, the wolf, and the donkey? You have at least heard of the rod; until not too long ago, learning was "taught to the tune of a hickory stick." Luther was acquainted with it at close quarters. One day, he recalled, he received fifteen strokes. The "wolf"—we might call him the class stool pigeon—was a student secretly appointed by the master to keep a record when anyone lapsed from Latin into German or used profanity. At the end of the week each demerit was paid off by one stroke of the switch. This is the explanation of Luther's rueful memory. The "donkey" was a wooden mask or carved symbol which the worst scholar in the class had to wear every morning at the end of the recitation; he could pass it to another pupil if he caught him speaking German.

Why all the emphasis on Latin? Latin was the key that opened the door to culture and to the learned professions. It spelled the difference between the professions and the trades. In those days only a minority of boys, and few girls, went to school. Peasant boys in the country picked up farming through their everyday work. In the villages and towns, apprenticeship was the way to learn a trade, whether you wanted to be a butcher, a baker, a barber, or a beggar.

School in Mansfeld

At Mansfeld, where Martin began school—perhaps at the age of four and a half—Latin grammar was the chief subject. It was not so much taught as pounded in. Luther later spoke of the schools as a "hell and purgatory in which we were tormented with cases and tenses, and yet learned less than nothing with all the flogging, trembling, anguish, and misery." But here as elsewhere he was exaggerating to score a point; he was then urging a radical reform of the school system. At Mansfeld and at his later schools he actually learned quite a bit. Though Latin may have been taught boringly and without regard for polished style, the grown-up Luther effort-lessly spoke and wrote this language of church and state, of learning and culture. In the rhetoric class, readings from classical Latin writers were chosen to teach morality and worldly wisdom. Memo-rization no doubt was deadly, but he remembered and used many of these passages throughout his life. Religious instruction, in word and music, played a large role. Youngsters learned mealtime prayers, the confession of sins, the Ten Commandments, the creed, the Lord's Prayer, the Hail Mary. Older schoolboys formed the choir which sang for church services and religious processions. They learned psalms and hymns from memory and heard the gospel and epistle lessons regularly. Here, no doubt, was laid the foundation of Luther's later mastery of the Latin Bible, huge sections of which he was able to reel off from memory. Martin's early years in school, moreover, were by no means all burden and boredom. With special delight he remembered, for instance, that in Mansfeld the big schoolboy, Nicolas Oemler, sometimes gave him rides on his shoulders. Nicolas later married Luther's sister.

At Magdeburg

In his fourteenth year Martin was sent to a school at Magdeburg. A city of twelve thousand and seat of an archbishop, Magdeburg broadened the youth's experience. Priests and monks were every-where. The most memorable to young Martin was a real prince, Wil-liam of Anhalt, who for the sake of his soul had become a monk, and could be seen, stooped over, a man of mere skin and bones, begging in the streets with a sack on his back. The boy thought it was the holiest sight he had ever seen. "Whoever looked upon him was deeply moved and felt ashamed of his worldly way of life," recalled Luther. Martin had among his teachers some Brothers of the Common Life. This devout fraternity, widespread in Holland and Germany, was composed mainly of laymen who lived in groups and gave themselves to worship, Bible reading, service, and especially to teaching.

Possibly it was in Magdeburg that Luther first saw a complete Bible. It is difficult to be sure, for there are several variations of this famous legend in *Table Talk*. One reference places the event in the Erfurt University library, another in the Erfurt monastery. Remem-ber, the narrators wrote at a time when Protestants were declaring that the Bible had been utterly unused and unknown before the Reformation. Luther had said something like this, but what he meant chiefly was that the Bible message had been encased in a teaching which utterly distorted it. Later Protestants added the fiction that the Bible was chained in place to prevent it from being read. Actually, the reason expensive books were chained in libraries and churches was because they were so much in demand.

As for Luther's discovery of the entire Bible, scholars now tend to credit the following account as the most reliable: "Once as a boy he happened on a Bible where by chance he read the story concerning the mother of Samuel. The book pleased him greatly and he thought he would be very fortunate if he should ever come to own such a book. Shortly afterward he bought a postil [at this time a postil meant a complete collection of the biblical lessons used in worship services]; this pleased him greatly because it contained more gospel passages than were usually taught during the course of the year. When he became a monk he gave up all his books. A short time before he had purchased the *Corpus Juris* and I do not know what other books. He sold them back to the book dealer, and took none of them with him into the monastery except Plautus and Virgil. There the monks gave him a Bible bound in red leather."

Beloved Eisenach

After a year in Magdeburg Martin transferred to the St. George School in Eisenach where, according to his friend Melanchthon, "he rounded out his Latin studies, and since he had a penetrating mind and rich gifts of expression, he soon outstripped his companions in eloquence, languages, and poetic verse." Luther was greatly impressed with the school. One teacher is said to have tipped his master's cap whenever he entered his classroom, in recognition that many distinguished citizens of the future might be among his students.

Luther had happy memories of experiences outside the classroom, too. Here, as at Magdeburg, he frequently sang in the streets for alms. This custom does not imply extreme poverty; one Luther expert has called it a sort of scholarship, another terms it "one of the milder forms of adolescent intimidation." A well-known, highly romanticized legend tells how a wealthy lady, Mrs. Cotta, took pity upon the poor student and welcomed him into her home. Apart from the exaggerations of the tale, Martin did, in any case, enjoy the hospitality of this cultured family, and he profited greatly from the strong religious convictions and the stimulating company of the Cottas and their guests. Eisenach was a happy place for Luther. He spoke of it as his "beloved town."

We can now look back upon Luther's first seventeen years. Can you look back on your own life, say at the age of ten, and recall your home relationships, your schooling, and your religious notions at that time? Can you then chart the development of your thinking from that day to the present? Using your own recollections as a rough measuring stick, is it not apparent that young Martin Luther had had a fairly normal life, with advantages and disadvantages, setbacks and successes, good times and bad? No convincing evidence exists from home and school that he was an unbalanced or maladjusted or rebellious boy. Nor did he show himself unusually brilliant in his progress, though we have found him an alert student. In brief, Luther was brought up in a home of conservative, average Catholic parents who were sincerely interested in their son, moderately well-to-do, and highly esteemed in their community. In school he received a training designed to nourish both his mental abilities and his loyalty to the church; there he earned respect as a good pupil.

7. Luther at Erfurt University

THE small-town boy's heart must have stirred with excitement when he walked to Erfurt to enroll as a university student in 1501. It was spring. He was seventeen. He must carve out a place for himself in the old and renowned university which had two thousand students, almost as many as the entire population of Eisleben or Eisenach. Erfurt itself was a fair-sized city, with perhaps twenty thousand inhabitants. Noted as a religious center, this "little Rome" boasted a hundred church institutions—"cathedral," churches, numerous monasteries, chapels, and hospitals.

University Life

Picture a strict, not too imaginative, religious prep school, and you will have a modernized version of university life in Erfurt. Luther lived in a hostel, or dormitory, rigidly supervised by a faculty member who had to certify not only a pupil's academic progress but also his moral integrity before he could earn a degree. Martin was expected to rise at 4 A.M. and retire at 8 P.M. Since artificial light was expensive, a university had to make the best possible use of daylight. A record was kept of the places where a student spent his time, and special permission was required to be out after dark. Daily devotions were prescribed in the dormitory, and religious works were read aloud during mealtime while the students ate silently.

The university curriculum likewise was strictly regimented. The instruction would correspond to our junior college level. First Luther studied advanced grammar, logic, and rhetoric—the precision tools of thought and verbal expression—although at Erfurt some general science also crept into the course. The ancient Greek philosopher Aristotle dominated the entire program. In the shortest possible time, three semesters, Luther earned his degree of Bachelor of Arts, placing thirtieth in a class of fifty-seven. He proceeded immediately to the advanced program traditionally consisting of arithmetic, geometry, music, and astronomy, which completed the "seven liberal arts." Actually the course at Erfurt embraced mathematics and general science, ethics (including politics), and metaphysics. A student's life was a busy round of lectures to be copied from dictation (in the infancy of printing, books were discouragingly expensive), the reading of assigned books, and periods of academic exercises, the most exciting of which was the weekly debate at 6 A.M. Of course students managed to find relaxation, too. Luther taught himself to play the lute, that day's counterpart to our guitar, and he was known as a "good fellow" among his friends. His roommate Crotus remembered him as "a musician and a learned philosopher."

Honors

In February, 1505, the twenty-one-year-old Luther received the august title of Master of Arts, ranking second in a class of seventeen —no mean achievement in the second best university in Germany. "It was a glorious and splendid time," Luther remembered, "when the successful candidates received their degrees. Torches were carried in front of them and tributes were paid to them. In my opinion there is no earthly pleasure known to man that equals it." Now he was ready to study with Germany's most eminent faculty of law. His father proudly began to address his son in the formal manner due to respected equals and superiors, and he provided the money for an expensive set of law books.

A few short months later, with a storm in his soul, Luther entered the Augustinian monastery at Erfurt, "dying to the world" and turning his back upon a promising law career and his father's favor.

8. Luther Enters the Monastery

LUTHER's enemies circulated a story that he had been a dissolute youth, and that he had entered the monastery to escape the consequences of his misdeeds. Though this tale was popular with his detractors until recently, no informed person credits it today. Did Luther have an abnormal tendency to melancholy, and did he make his vow during a fit of despondency? This charge is more difficult to judge. Certainly he had an unusual sensitivity to the seriousness of sin, but whether it amounted to an abnormal tendency to melancholy may better be decided after we have examined Luther's life in full.

Did he simply feel that he was not cut out for a career in law? Perhaps, but he also said that he had not felt cut out for a monastic career: "Not eagerly did I become a monk."

But though the vow was unplanned, it was not unprepared. Because of the way Luther had been brought up, it was a perfectly normal decision. Indeed, one of the church's great holy men, St. Norbert, had been called to the monastic life in exactly the same fashion—by a thunderbolt. If the vow seems abnormal to us today, it is largely because Protestants agree with Luther's later sharp criticism of the whole monastic system. To a Roman Catholic, however, the abnormal thing would not be vowing to enter a monastery, but deciding to leave it.

Vivid events had made a deep impression upon the university student, for he remembered them long afterward. Once after starting a journey home, he accidentally cut a deep gash in his leg with the short dagger which students wore. While his companion hurried back to Erfurt for help, Martin lay in danger of bleeding to death. "Help, Mary!" he cried. Not long before his vow, a good friend at the university died. Luther later recalled that he felt depressed and restless for some time.

Events such as these helped to force upon his attention what the church had been teaching all the time: Life is brief and uncertain; God's dreaded judgment is near; even one mortal sin unabsolved at death is enough to condemn me to writhe in hell forever. God requires me to love him above all else; but even with all his grace to me, have I really done this? Luther later said repeatedly that he had been terrified when he saw Christ portrayed sternly sitting upon a rainbow, ready to separate the damned from the saved. How could a man get God to be gracious to him? Would anyone be so foolish as to ignore all the help that the church had to offer?

Among the church's helps, none could match the monastic life. Though one could live a holy life within the world, monasticism was the Christian way of life par excellence. Through the triple vow of poverty, chastity, and obedience, a monk devoted himself unreservedly to the service of Christ. In poverty he forsook the distractions of possessions. In chastity he renounced the distractions of family life. In obedience he crushed his self-will and lived a life of humility and self-denial. Noting Jesus' expression in Matthew 5, "You have heard that it was said. . . . But I say to you. . . " the church had drawn a distinction between Christ's commandments and his "counsels of perfection." The former are the minimum requirements for reaching heaven; the latter are the higher righteousness, the "second mile" of Christian faithfulness and love. While ordinary Christians should try to obey the "counsels," the monk bound himself to fulfill them always. Accordingly the monastic life was commonly called "the state of perfection." Surely the monk was the most devoted and complete servant of Christ, and the monastic life the surest way to salvation. On becoming a monk a man is as if newly baptized, once again as innocent and pure as at the moment when he was first lifted out of the font. Little wonder, then, that in terror of death young Martin Luther sought the "haven of the cowl." His later remarks confirm that his reasons for entering the monastery were "to serve God," to "perform the great obedience," to "save his soul," to "escape hell."

Try to imagine yourself in young Martin's place. What alternatives were open, once he had cried out in the storm? He could quietly forget the vow; no one had heard him. But he was not the kind to forget it. And God had heard it. He might rationalize his fright and explain it away as a relic of superstition. But what if this lightning bolt was a sign from God? He could obtain a release; a vow made under duress is not binding. True, he felt that the vow had been wrung from him, but what if it had been wrung by God? He could make the best of the vow and still work out a pleasant life. The vow at Stotternheim bound him only to give the monastic life a trial; this was the purpose of the novice year. Even if he went through with his permanent vow, he might seek promotion to power or a life of scholarship. But Luther sought no favors, and among the six monasteries in Erfurt, he deliberately chose a strict one. There could be no easy way to win peace with God.

Only one thing really counted to Martin. He had to enter the monastery to save his soul. God was driving him. So the graduate student sold his law books. He entertained his closest friends in the evening, and on the next day, July 17, 1505, parted from them at the entrance to the cloister of the Order of St. Augustine, an order of monks commonly called Augustinians. The gates closed behind him. "I never considered leaving the monastery. I had become purely dead to the world."

9. Monk, Priest, and Teacher

"OH, when will you ever become good, and do enough to win a gracious God?" This nagging question that Luther asked himself drove him into the monastery; it was the question that spurred him to strenuous efforts in following the monastic way of life.

The question with its odd expressions seems strange, doesn't it? "When will you become good?" Luther's term is usually translated "pious," but primarily, in his day, it meant upright, faithful, having integrity—"good" in the fullest and best sense. A "gracious" God? Not socially gracious, of course, but a God who is pleased with me, who treats me with favor and acceptance, in contrast to an angry, rejecting God. "Win" God's favor—induce God to be favorable to me? How odd. If God is love, isn't he always favorable? No, Luther would answer even after his "discovery of the gospel"—not just because of his medieval training, but because the Scriptures say no. God is love, but his love is holy love, with a place for real wrath and real judgment. Beware taking God's grace for granted. It is nothing cheap. How are we to gain God's favor? "Do enough"? For Luther this was the rub.

Luther's worried mood is not easy to understand. Modern people who are not even sure whether there is a God feel remote from a Luther who was so certain that there is. Persons who amiably welcome religion as long as they don't have to take it too seriously are perplexed at a Luther who found this question so difficult that he suffered a kind of breakdown. Even those who take their faith seriously may be baffled at Luther's trouble. Is God so hard to please? We must beware whittling God's holiness down to our size. But thousands had found this monastic way satisfactory. Luther knew it; it made his later decision all the more difficult.

In any case, the quest for a gracious God remained the dominant passion of his entire life. It is the thread that we must follow throughout his career. As we shall see, Luther became a reformer, not by dropping the question he had first asked, but by refashioning it.

In the Monastery

When Luther first entered the monastery, however, the old question seemed right and the prospects of satisfaction excellent. After several weeks under observation, he was initiated as a novice at an impressive ceremony. He prostrated himself before the prior. "What do you seek?" asked the prior. "God's grace and your mercy," replied Luther. The candidate was raised from the floor and asked whether he was married, under personal obligations, or diseased. Then the prior described the severity of the monastic life and inquired whether Luther was ready to undergo all these hardships. "Yes, with God's help, in so far as human frailty permits." While the brothers sang a hymn, Luther was clothed in a monk's habit—a white hooded robe or cowl and a white scapular, a strip of material like a long stole, signifying the yoke of Christ. For official and outside garb he would wear over the white garments a black hooded mantle with a leather sash. Then his hair was clipped. After the ceremony his head would be tonsured, leaving a ring of hair symbolic of the crown of thorns.

Strict and strenuous was the life now expected of him, as he was told during the ceremony: renunciation of self-will, scant diet and rough clothing, vigils by night and labors by day, discipline of the flesh, willingness to bear the reproach of poverty and the shame of begging and the disgust for the monastic life that might sweep over him. Now under a good master of novices, he learned by experience what this meant. He was taught how to conduct himself on all occasions—at the seven-times-daily worship services, at table, even when alone. He had to learn how to walk with his eyes always downcast, how to keep silence in the corridors and in his bare, unheated, seven-by ten-foot cell. He learned humility by humiliation, such as begging and working on the clean-up detail. He learned how to discipline his body and exalt his soul; extra prayers and vigils, extra fasts, and scourging were approved ways.

All this training Luther readily accepted. It was hard, but he had entered the cloister to learn holiness and this was the church's age-old recommendation. Protestants need not deride the monastic ideal. It was no mere retreat from the world. If the miseries of this world and man's inhumanity to man all stem from the powers of evil, the monks were in special training to fight these powers. Nor need Protestants imagine that this ideal was dead. Though many monasteries were disgracefully faithless, as we know from contemporary sources, the Augustinian convent at Erfurt was not. The district vicar, Father von Staupitz, had seen to that. A strict new constitution and conscientious discipline were in force.

At Last a Monk

The novice year rolled by quickly. In September, 1506, Luther was ready for the irrevocable decision. Nothing had persuaded him to change his mind, not even his father's violent anger over the vow. For had not Christ said, "He who loves father or mother more than me is not worthy of me" (Matthew 10:37)? The final decision, meanwhile, was not Luther's alone, but required also the explicit approval of the monastic brothers who had watched him as a novice. But he had no problem there. They were satisfied that he had the holy calling.

"Dear brother," the prior addressed the kneeling candidate, "your probationary year is over. You have experienced the strictness of our order. Now you must choose one of two courses: either to part from us, or else to renounce the world and consecrate yourself utterly, first to God, and secondly to our Order. Moreover, after you have thus offered yourself, you dare not for any reason shake the yoke of obedience off your neck." Luther was ready. He received a newly consecrated cowl, signifying innocence and world-renouncing humility. With his hands on a copy of the Augustinian Rule, Luther made the permanently binding vow. "If you keep this," responded the prior, "I promise you eternal life." A procession, more prayers and blessings, and the brothers' solemn kiss of peace completed the ceremony. Luther was now a monk, as innocent as a newly baptized child, and fortified with all the merits that the Augustinian Order had accumulated.

And Then a Priest

He was immediately marked for higher responsibilities in the order. Not too often did a man of Luther's academic rank enter a monastery. The order directed him to prepare for the priesthood. For this he did not need a long theological course but only a brief guided-study program, for the basic task of a priest was simply to exercise the supernatural gift of "power and discretion" which he received through the bishop at ordination. "Power" meant the ability to "sacrifice Christ" on the altar during the Mass. According to the church's teachings, the priest performed the miracle of changing the bread and wine, despite all outward appearances, into the true body and blood of the Savior. "Discretion" meant the ability to administer the Sacrament of Penance: to hear private confession, to declare the forgiveness of mortal sins, and to impose the penalties ("satisfactions") designed to prove the penitent's sincerity and repair the order of justice which the sin had damaged. Indeed, not all priests had to hear confession; many had no official public duty but to recite a specified number of Masses endowed by pious persons to win God's favor or to help release some departed soul from purgatory. To prepare for ordination, then, Luther was assigned to read Gabriel Biel's long book on the Canon of the Mass; formal theological study could come later.

But if the priest's basic task seemed simple in one sense, in reality his was the most awesome responsibility on earth. The priest dispensed or withheld God's grace, by which alone man could win salvation and escape hell. Only the priest could perform the Mass, which presented Christ's sacrifice on Calvary once again to God and thus pleased God and kept his grace coming afresh into his church. Only the priest could declare to a repentant sinner that his mortal sin was forgiven. The Mass and the Sacrament of Penance were the twin centers of medieval religion, and the priest alone had charge of both. In Biel's great book—almost a whole course in "practical theology"—Luther read that the dignity of the priest outshines the splendor of kings as gold outshines lead, for kings bow their necks to priests. Priests are exalted above all laymen as heaven is higher than earth. At the privilege of the priest, heaven is amazed and earth marvels, man fears and hell shudders, the Devil trembles and the angelic host worships fervently. To him belongs power not granted even to angels or to the Blessed Virgin Mary. No wonder Luther recalled, "When I read that book, my heart bled!"

Soon came the wonderful day of his ordination, April 4, 1507. Still more exciting was the second of May, for on this day he would celebrate his first Mass, he would perform the awesome miracle of sacrificing Christ. Hans Luther had softened, to the extent that he attended the celebration and gave twenty gulden to the monastery—a handsome sum in a day when three gulden would buy a fatted ox.

Luther took his place at the altar and began the sacred rite. Once more the old anxieties over his unworthiness before God began to build up within him. "Who am I, that I should lift up my eyes or raise my hands to the divine Majesty? The angels surround him. At his nod the earth trembles. And shall I, a miserable little pygmy, say

44

'I want this, I ask for that'? For I am dust and ashes and full of sin, yet I am speaking to the living, eternal and true God!" His celebration would be effective whether he was personally holy or not. But a priest in the state of sin was forbidden to officiate at the altar; he who consecrates ought to be "worthy." How could he really know what lay at the depths of his heart?

He approached the very moment when the wafer of bread, uplifted in his hands, would cease to be bread and would become Christ's own body. "I was so horrified that I would have run away from the altar if the prior had not admonished me. For when I read the words of the Canon, 'Therefore, most gracious Father,' and I was aware that I had to speak directly with God himself without a mediator, I wanted to flee as Judas fled from the world." Once more, though only within his heart, the lightning had struck.

He pulled himself together and finished. Later at a festive meal with the brothers and his guests, he could relax and rejoice. But he who had trembled at the majesty of the heavenly Father now craved a word of approval from his earthly father. Aren't you satisfied now with the course I have taken? Besides, I did not plan this. Terrors from heaven forced me to become a monk. Hans Luther growled, "Just so it was not a delusion of the devil!" Martin remembered these words for the rest of his life. But at the same time he was full of the happy glow of his holy position. He gently chided his father for having been angry. Hans suddenly flared up. "Have you never read, 'Honor your father and your mother'?" There was the rub. The Fourth Commandment was clear Scripture, the voice of God himself; in comparison, how could he be sure that the vow in the storm was God's call, and not a trick of the Devil to lure him to his destruction?

Assignment to Teach

Luther's next assignment was to study philosophy and theology in order to teach. The Augustinian Order placed a high value on learning. It needed not only good priests but also instructors for its own school program, and some Augustinians held regular positions in the university's theological faculty. Monks could hear lectures both at the university and in their cloister. Brother Martin accordingly began his climb through the ranks of the graduate school, meanwhile serving as an instructor on the faculty of liberal arts.

Now he had to delve into the deepest riddles that plague men's hearts and minds. How much can we learn about God and his world simply by using our human reason, and how much of this truth must

God reveal through Scripture? To what extent can man become truly good by developing the moral virtues, and to what extent does he need divine grace for this end? In what sense does God predestine a man to salvation or rejection, and to what degree does a man's own free will make the difference? How do the sacraments convey God's grace, and how do human churchmen control the divine sacraments?

Luther's progress was swift and his teaching tasks were increased. In the fall of 1508 he was suddenly transferred to Wittenberg University to lecture for a year on Aristotle's ethics, and then brought back to Erfurt to lecture on theology, all the while continuing his own studies. His fantastic memory helped him; he could repeat most of Biel and a few other theologians by heart. More significantly, he could do the same with his Latin Bible. He had put the red-bound Bible to heavy use ever since it was given to him. Somewhere along the line Luther formed the habit of reading through the entire Bible twice a year.

10. The Storms of the Soul

AFTER five years in the monastery, Luther was successful, if success is measured in terms of promotion within an organization. Still in his twenties, he showed promise of rising high in the Augustinian Order. He was successful, too, in the reputation he had won for spiritual earnestness. Even men who remained Roman Catholic at the great splintering testified that Brother Martin had been an irreproachable monk and actually "a second Paul."

But real success does not necessarily show up in records and reputations. It is not only what a person does and how he appears, but what he really is. Luther could think of success only in terms of what he actually was before God. He believed firmly in the scriptural insight, "For the LORD sees not as man sees; man looks on the outward appearance, but the LORD looks on the heart" (1 Samuel 16:7).

Half a lifetime later, Luther said, "I also have been a monk, and so tortured myself with prayers, fastings, vigils, and freezing that I almost died of cold, which hurt me so much that I would never want to do it again even if I could. What else did I seek but God? I wanted him to see how well I kept the rule of the order and how strict a life I led. Thus I lived constantly in a delusion and sheer idolatry. For I did not believe in Christ, but regarded him only as a stern, horrible judge, as he is pictured sitting on a rainbow. Therefore I turned to other intercessors, Mary and other saints, also to my own works and the merits of my Order. All this I did not for the sake of money and possessions but for the sake of God. Nevertheless, it was all false religion and idolatry, because I did not know Christ and did not seek these goals in him and through him."

But Luther was not perpetually unhappy. Once he remarked that "the devil is quiet during a person's first year as a monk or a priest." At times he was proud of the "precious way of life" and thought that he was "walking on the right path straight toward heaven."

Luther was not satisfied simply to get by. He had the thoroughness and drive of a champion in a contest where the stakes are high. "I wanted to offer myself body and soul to our Lord God," Luther remembered. "I wanted to make God justify me on account of my works and my rigorous life." Indeed, a holy person could not only win his own salvation but also help to save others. If the monastic way was really right, then the more fervently he followed it, the purer, more pleasing, more placid his own life should be.

Ways to Holiness

Luther's advisers recommended three ways to attain personal holiness. These could be combined in various fashions. The first was the way of moral achievement. By strictly obeying the rule and by sternly disciplining his body and mind, he should be able to become free of all selfishness and become a pure vessel to adore God and serve mankind. "I tried with all the diligence I could muster to fulfill all the regulations, lashing my body with hunger, vigils, prayers, and other exercises, laying a greater burden upon it than it could bear without endangering my health." "Frequently I took not a morsel or a drop for three days." He said Mass daily and devoted himself to other pious works. So well did he do that at times he "felt completely holy from head to heel." He could say to himself, "Today I have committed no sin. I have obeyed my prior, and I have fasted and prayed. Therefore, may God be gracious to me!"

Some churchmen recommended another way for certain individuals. They taught mysticism, a technique to lift the soul above all earthly things. A devout person, having "purified" himself by devotional, moral, and intellectual effort, might hope to receive a divine "illumination" which would flood his soul with radiance. Finally, he might on occasion be granted the supreme ecstasy of feeling actually "united" with God. With this prescription, too, Luther enjoyed some

success: "Once I was caught up into the third heaven." "I thought I was among the choirs of angels."

The third way, intercession, was especially useful when a person could not trust that his record with God was all it should be. The saints, said the church, have done more good works than they themselves need to merit God's favor. God therefore has reserved their merits to be given to those who invoke the saints' aid. The Virgin Mary and the saints intercede with Christ, the holy judge, to turn away his wrath upon sinners. Particular saints help a man in particular needs. Accordingly, Luther selected twenty-one saints and prayed to three each day as he celebrated Mass, completing the round in a week. And in the monastic order itself, the merits which the holy monks had accumulated were shared by all the brothers.

In all the ways to holiness Luther seemed successful. "But though I was greatly pleased," he said, "with the sweet praises and fine words describing me as a 'miracle-worker' who had made himself holy with so little effort, everything fell apart."

Inner Struggle

For all his religious efforts, Luther could not feel that he had eliminated the impurity within him. Most people regard impurity as a problem of the flesh. Luther's concern was much deeper. "In the monastery my thoughts were preoccupied with neither money nor this world's goods nor women." Temptations of the spirit, not of the body, assailed him. The Ten Commandments begin by forbidding us to put anything above or even equal to God, and end by forbidding us to covet—a word which Luther understood to include evil desire in any form. "Each time I experienced evil desires, such as anger, hatred, jealousy toward a brother, I tried all kinds of remedies. I confessed daily, but the evil desire always returned. This is why I could find no peace but was perpetually in torment, thinking: 'You have committed this or that sin. In vain have you joined the Order. All your good works are useless.'"

In such a mood he felt unworthy to receive the Lord's Supper. He dreaded God's coming judgment. Worse still, he even came to hate the God who would summon him to judgment. "In thy righteousness deliver me!" said Psalm 31:1. But a righteous God will not deliver the unrighteous; he hates sinners. God's gospel is a power for salvation and it reveals his righteousness, says Romans 1:16–17, so that the righteous man shall live by faith. Of course, but what about the unrighteous? Why, "the wrath of God is revealed from heaven against all ungodliness and wickedness of men . . . " (1:18).

"Blessed are all who take refuge in him," sings Psalm 2:11, but first it demands: "Serve the LORD with fear, with trembling kiss his feet, lest he be angry, . . . for his wrath is quickly kindled."

To hate God, in turn, was blasphemy and rebellion. God must have rejected him forever. Perhaps these assaults upon his conscience came not only from the Devil but from God himself.

Luther's trouble was by no means new. The medieval church considered itself well equipped to relieve men who had barbs in their consciences. It had a great body of literature dealing with peace of mind or soul. Best of all, it had the great Sacrament of Penance through which to counsel the troubled soul and to apply the healing medicine of divine grace.

Luther, who as a priest heard confession, himself sought grace and counsel with feverish earnestness. Through stretches of time he confessed daily. Once he remained in the confessional for six hours and ransacked his memory for all his sins of thought and word and deed from his youth on.

What should his confessors say to this hypersensitive soul? "Don't talk so much!" was the rebuke from one wornout priest. Another admonished him, "God is not angry with you; you are angry with God!" They were both correct, Luther admitted. Should the confessors reprove him for being anxious about his guilt? No, an activated conscience was in itself a good thing; confessors more commonly had to wrestle with the dull or hardened conscience. But this young monk seemed overanxious.

Sometimes the church's medicine helped Luther, but it brought him no lasting relief. "Be moderate in your self-discipline," he was told; "Maltreating your body is itself a sin." Yes, but the commentary on our rule also says: "Woe to the monk who loves his health more than holiness!" "According to the Creed we believe in the forgiveness of sins." "Despair is a deadly sin. God has commanded you to hope!" Yes, but no one dare hope without merits; your words do not apply to me. "Don't worry so much over God's justice; think of his mercy." Yes, but God has said, "You shall be holy; for I the LORD your God am holy" (Leviticus 19:2); "Return to me, says the LORD of hosts, and I will return to you" (Zechariah 1:3); "Seek, and you will find" (Luke 11:9); therefore do the best you can, and God will not deny you grace. But this is just the trouble. Am I really turning to God and seeking him, or am I talking out of both sides of my mouth at once? Unconfessed sins are not forgiven, unless they are unintentionally forgotten; but if I forget them, am I not forgetting intentionally? In his Latin Bible, at Ecclesiastes 9:1, Luther read words which summed up all his uncertainty—man knows not whether he is worthy of love or hatred.

"Under all my holiness and self-confidence I nourished a perpetual mistrust, doubt, fear, hatred, and blasphemy of God," Luther later recalled. "With all my masses, prayers, fasts, vigils, and chastity, I never reached the point where I could say, 'Now I am sure that I please God,' or 'Now I know from experience that my Order and my austere life have helped me progress toward heaven.'" Consequently, "the more I worked to heal my wavering, weak, afflicted conscience by means of human teachings, the more wavering, weak and disturbed I made it." At times God seemed to him a tyrant, and Christ a hangman. The monastery seemed a prison, a slaughterhouse, a steam bath. "There in the convent I was the most wretched man on earth, passing whole days and nights in weeping and despairing of help."

But he was still convinced that being a monk was the surest way to heaven.

11. The Visit to Rome

THOUGH lightning was flashing within his soul, it seems that the storm rarely burst into the open. In any case the outward career of the earnest monk was advancing smoothly. At Wittenberg University he had lectured and won his first degree in theology. Now, in connection with a touchy case of monastic business, Luther was selected to take a trip to Rome.

Authorities in Rome had approved a plan of Dr. von Staupitz, head of the stricter branch of the German Augustinians, to tighten up the administration of the entire order. The plan proved unpopular, however, and not only with the lax cloisters. Some of the stricter ones determined to present a protest at Rome. Young Brother Martin was named the junior member of a two-man delegation to the Holy City.

But to visit Rome, too, the capital of Christendom, hallowed with the blood of so many martyrs, enriched with so many sacred relics! What enormous good this pilgrimage would do for his soul. It was hard to decide what thrilled the young monk more—the assignment to help handle such a delicate affair, or the opportunity to visit holy Rome, the center of the Christian world.

Late in the autumn of 1510 Luther and his companion set out on their long walk over the Alps. At twenty-five miles a day they spent the best part of two months on the road. At last Luther caught his first glimpse of the city. Flooded with emotion he prostrated himself on the ground and cried, "Hail, holy Rome!"

With fewer than fifty thousand inhabitants, the shabby medieval city was a mere shell of its ancient imperial glory. But Luther wasted no nostalgia upon the humbled, crumbled empire. There were holy sights to be seen and holy benefits to be collected. Like "a madman full of religious zeal," he raced to visit churches and catacombs. Such fabulous relics, all too genuine to be doubted. He saw relics from Christ's passion: thorns from his crown, the rope, the sponge, Pilate's inscription, a nail and some wood from the cross, water and blood from Christ's side. He saw Moses' rod and some pieces of the burning bush, two fragments of the loaves Jesus used in feeding the five thousand, and some milk of the Virgin Mary. Viewing one of Judas' pieces of silver brought him a valuable indulgence: fourteen thousand years' reduction of his time in purgatory. Kissing two crosses at the spot where Peter's and Paul's relics were kept brought him seventeen thousand years' indulgence.

One pious desire remained unfulfilled. Brother Martin had hoped to see His Holiness in person. But Pope Julius and most of his cardinals were off in northern Italy, fighting a war against the French.

Luther said so many Masses that he lost count. At some altars a single Mass could release a soul from purgatory. He almost regretted that his father and mother were still alive, for he would have liked to have them obtain this benefit. However, his grandfather was dead, and to liberate his soul Luther climbed up "Pilate's Stairs" on his knees, praying an "Our Father" on each medieval stone step. A well-known legend, circulated several decades later by Luther's son Paul, relates that while he was praying, he remembered, "The just shall live by faith," and he turned around and walked down. Luther himself tells a different story: "When I reached the top I kept thinking: Who knows whether this is true!"

The earnest German monk brought home from his trip some dismal impressions of the condition of the church. He was appalled at the slick professionalism of the Italian priests who could run through several Masses in the time it took him to say one, and who angrily muttered, "Get a move on!" as he celebrated the holy rite. He was shocked to hear that there were cynical priests who recited in the sacred liturgy of the Mass, "Bread you are and bread you will

53

remain,"—knowing that common people, after all, could not understand the Latin words. Corruption in high places was notorious, and immorality was fairly well taken for granted even in popes and other high churchmen. No wonder the rumor was abroad that Rome was situated directly above hell.

Yet Luther returned to Erfurt, after five months' absence, still an ardently loyal son of the Roman Catholic church.

12. Doctor and Professor

As for the petition of the seven monasteries, it was turned down. But despite the fact that Luther had been a spokesman for the opposition, within half a year after his return from Rome, Vicar Staupitz was grooming him for important promotions within the order.

The explanation is not hard to find. Once the papal authorities had announced their decision, Luther and his friend John Lang accepted it. They began to feel that perhaps Staupitz's plan was good after all, though many of their fellow monks at Erfurt and elsewhere continued their furious opposition. In the summer of 1511 Staupitz therefore transferred Luther and Lang to Wittenberg.

As the vicar and young Brother Martin came to know each other better, they discovered many common interests. The study of the Bible in their day was widely regarded as a subject for beginners, since up-to-date theologians presumably had extracted from it whatever was valuable for the church. Staupitz was pleased that Luther, on the contrary, dug back into the Scriptures whenever he pondered the problems of the Christian faith. Again, most German theologians emphasized how much men can do to merit their salvation; Luther, like Staupitz, placed the primary emphasis on God's grace—what God does to save men from their wickedness and waywardness, their pride and their despair. Luther, in turn, found the vicar as deeply concerned as he was with the question of how a person can get right with God. More and more the young monk poured out his own problem to his superior, and the vicar gave him a sympathetic hearing and wise counsel.

New Fields of Service

Here, thought Staupitz, was a young brother with a leader's potential who might relieve him of some of his excessive responsibilities.

Surely the vicar had enough to do, supervising twenty-nine monasteries and also serving as professor of Bible at Wittenberg University. One day in September, as the two were sitting under a pear tree in the monastery garden, Staupitz broke the news that Luther should take up the office of preaching; further, he should earn his doctorate and succeed the vicar as professor of Bible. "This will give you something to do," he smiled. Luther was aghast. He listed fifteen reasons why he could not possibly meet the assignment. "Besides," he protested, "it will kill me!" "That's all right," replied the vicar amiably. "God has a lot of business to handle. If you die, you can become one of his advisers!"

That settled it. A monk had no choice but to obey his superior. Martin immediately set to work to earn the doctor's degree at Wittenberg. Promotions in monastic duties, meanwhile, hardly helped him concentrate on his graduate studies. First he was appointed a preacher in the monastery, then in the spring of 1512 the order elected him sub-prior (second in command) at Wittenberg, which made him instructor of novices. Even so, he completed his studies handily. On October 19, 1512, in a ceremony full of solemn pomp, Luther took the doctor's oath, swearing loyalty to the faculty and promising not to teach vain or strange doctrines which were condemned by the church and offensive to pious ears. A doctor's cap was placed on his head and a silver-mounted golden doctor's ring on his finger. Fellow students carried Dr. Luther in a parade through the streets and the town bell rang to honor this rare distinction.

In retrospect, what an irony appears in this doctoral promotion. Luther had promised to teach nothing contrary to the church. The church itself had charged him to open the Bible to the people of his day. This he would continue to do faithfully, even after he discovered that it meant criticizing the church of his day. When assailants accused him of heresy and arrogance for defying the authorities, Luther cleared his conscience. "I, Dr. Martin," he wrote in 1531, "was called and forced to become a doctor, with no thanks to me, out of sheer obedience. I had to assume the office of doctor and take an oath and vow to my beloved holy scriptures, to preach and teach them faithfully and purely."

The Professor

In 1512, however, neither Luther nor his friends yet foresaw the coming clash. Three days after his promotion he was installed in the theological faculty of Wittenberg University as Professor of Holy Scripture, succeeding Staupitz. Not bad for a young man of twenty-eight. At Erfurt, remarked Dr. Luther later (with a little exaggeration), one had to be fifty to receive a doctorate.

At six o'clock one morning in August, 1513, the new professor began his first biblical course: "Good fathers and brothers, I see you have come with a large and kindly spirit to do honor to the famous prophet David." Luther had chosen to teach the Book of Psalms, that familiar treasure of the church's devotion.

From the first, these lectures attracted attention. For one thing they were marked by diligent preparation. The young professor had carefully consulted Augustine and more than half a dozen "standard" authors. Then he had boldly used his own judgment. Still extant are most of his handwritten notes for this course; they fill over eleven hundred large pages in the printed edition. In those days of few books, when professors dictated their lectures word for word, Luther could use only a fraction of his material, even though he continued the twice-weekly class for two whole years.

There was also a progressive note in the lectures which good students appreciated. Luther had assembled the best Latin text of the Psalms, and the university printer had published it on large pages with lines wide apart and huge margins so that students could jot down comments right at the most convenient spot. Moreover Luther had prepared helpful summaries which were printed at the head of each psalm.

Though droning Latin dictation could have been deadly dull, something about the professor's style fired the students' interest. Many years later a violent opponent of Luther remembered his impression of those lectures: "The students heard him gladly, for they had never listened to anyone like him, who so boldly translated every Latin word into German." Partly, this was a tribute to the vividness of Luther's words. Even more, it was due to the lecturer's drive not merely to sound "learned," but to make the Bible become alive in the hearts of his hearers. In every psalm, in every verse, what is God saying to us? Here was a teacher who, like Jacob in the Old Testament, wrestled with the living God and would not give up until he had won a blessing.

13. *From Breakdown to Breakthrough*

MONK with a reputation for holiness, then Doctor of Holy Scripture, now successful teacher and rising leader in the order—this does not sound like a great storm brewing. From Luther's later recollections, however, we can chart the course of a fearful inward ordeal.

Through the teaching in which he had been trained, he says, "I lost Christ as a Savior and Comforter and made him a jailer and hangman of my poor soul. Now we have the light again. But when I became a doctor, I did not know the truth about him."

Next the recurring experiences of despair: "However blamelessly I lived as a monk, I felt that in God's presence I was a sinner with a most uneasy conscience, nor could I trust that he was appeased by my works of satisfaction. I did not love this God who punished sinners. Indeed, I hated him and raged at him." "More than once I was at the abyss of despair, so that I wished I had never been born." When he was in the pit of despair, he went to his most helpful counselors, but at this point they had to admit, "I don't understand you." "Fine comfort!" Luther recalled. "I thought, nobody experiences this kind of attack but myself. I felt like a corpse!" "Why does God pick on me alone?" Though Luther himself does not date these incidents, we may use them to describe the climax of his inward battle.

Finally, however, came the discovery in the monastery tower at Wittenberg that changed everything, the new insight into God in whose presence he stood: "I felt that I was completely reborn, that I had entered paradise itself through open gates."

Here in brief are three checkpoints of the supreme crisis in Luther's way to the gospel. Luther experienced a real breakdown, but one of an unusual kind. He did not need to be taken away for a time to regain his health; indeed, he apparently did not even interrupt his work in university and monastery. These incidents show that the breakthrough to the gospel, which made of Luther a new man and eventually the great reformer, was an answer to his own intense inward struggle to be right with God. Finally, though the breakthrough seems to have been dramatically sudden, Luther's spiritual growth really proceeded slowly, over a period of many years.

As we have already seen, the pressure was mounting within Luther as he tried to make sure that he pleased God. It should not surprise us that the storm in his soul did not reach its peak until after his doctoral promotion. One reason he worked so intensely on Scripture, graduate study, and his biblical lectures, was that his intense personal struggle was not yet resolved.

Two Questions

Luther was wrestling with two enormous questions. First, who am I, Martin Luther? Is it possible for a man to be completely honest about himself? A conscience has no standard, built-in gauge; your conscience can be either sharpened or blunted, as you wish. Men can adjust their consciences by cutting God down to their size. Luther in his Psalms lectures pictured them saying: "Oh, why are you so worried? Do you think God requires such strict conduct from you? He knows your limitations, and he is good. One groan will please him." Even theologians liked to say, "Do your best, and God will not deny you grace." Against all these maneuverings, asked Luther, can a man recognize, not only in his bad moments, but even in his best deeds, that he simply is not pure in the presence of a pure and holy God?

Second, who is this God in whose presence I must live? How does he deal with men? Here, too, we have already seen the storm clouds gathering. They converged on the idea of God's justice or righteousness. Justice, the philosophers had taught Luther, is the virtue of "giving every man what is due him." Applied to God, this meant the quality "by which God himself is just, and damns the wicked." This view could only make the earnest monk despair. As he recalled later, "Formerly when I prayed the verse of Psalm 31, 'In thy righteousness deliver me,' I was altogether terrified, and I hated that word from the bottom of my heart. 'Oh no, dear God,' I thought, 'not thy righteousness, but in thy mercy!'"

Actually Christianity in Luther's day had not forgotten that God is a God of grace, who gives righteousness to his children. But according to its common teachings, God's grace was still enveloped in a justice system. He gave grace, indeed, but this was to help men win merits so that at the Last Judgment they could satisfy his justice. In the last resort man was still left with the need to earn God's acceptance.

When a monk confessed his sins, this was the absolution or forgiveness he received: "May the merit of the passion of our Lord Jesus Christ, of Blessed and Ever Virgin Mary, and of all the saints, the merit of your Order, the humility of your confession and the contrition of your heart, the good works that you have done and will do for love of our Lord Jesus Christ—may all this bring you the forgiveness of sins. . . ." When Luther recalled this "conditional absolution," he raged, "But who in the world can claim that he has produced enough contrition and sorrow for his sin?" No wonder he saw God as a "judge and tyrant," and "felt nauseated" when he heard the word "justice."

Spiritual Attacks

Over him again and again swept the agonizing experience of God's wrath which he could not turn aside. Again and again came the stings of his own conscience from which he could not run away. No doubt there was more than just a dash of morbidity in Luther's mood. Still, the crucial point is that he was wrestling with no figment of his imagination, but with the living God. It was a life-or-death battle.

Luther gave a colorful name to these troubles. Perhaps "temptation" has become too tame a word, for it generally conjures up the picture of a wicked act that we are enticed to commit or a duty we are dared to evade. For Luther, however, the power that caused these torments was not passive but violently aggressive. Accordingly he called them "assaults" or "attacks," for he pictured a man stormed or besieged by a deadly enemy—the Devil, or perhaps God himself. One can seek strength against them, one can fight back, but when they really overcome a man, he cannot control them, else they would be mere exercises and not genuine assaults.

"I knew a man," he wrote in 1518 (probably meaning himself), "who claimed that he often suffered these pains, spanning a very brief period of time, but so intense and so hellish that neither tongue nor pen can describe nor can anyone believe who has not experienced them; if they lasted a half an hour, or even a tenth part of an hour, he would utterly perish and his bones would be reduced to ashes. At such a time God appears horribly angry, and the whole creation with him. There is no escape, no comfort within or without, only accusation from all sides. Then he laments, 'I am driven far from thy sight' (Psalm 31:22), yet he does not even dare to say, 'Lord, rebuke me not in thy anger' (Psalm 6:1). In this moment, strange to tell, the soul cannot believe it can ever be redeemed. All that is left is the naked desire for help and a dreadful groan, but it knows not where to seek help. Here the soul is stretched out with Christ so that 'all his bones can be counted' (Psalm 22:17), and every corner of it is filled with the most intense bitterness, horror, dread, and dejection, and all these seem eternal."

Throughout his life these "spiritual attacks" occupied an important place in Luther's own faith and in his counsel to men in need. Once he remarked, "Without these attacks nobody can understand the scriptures, or know the fear and love of God; indeed, one cannot know the Holy Spirit." Significantly, the assaults did not disappear forever once he "found the gospel."

Seeking Help

The young monk and professor sought help wherever he could. Counselors helped sometimes and many books offered him useful insights. But none brought his new understanding of the gospel to birth; at most they were "midwives" assisting at its birth.

His best helper in the midst of his attacks was his superior and good friend, Dr. Staupitz. The vicar did not claim to understand Luther's experiences of despair, "but," he said, "they seem more necessary to you than food and drink." Staupitz, however, did understand some important things about spiritual attacks which genuinely helped Brother Martin. Luther's torments brought two problems into focus: predestination and repentance. Were not his despair and blasphemy a sign that God had rejected him and destined him for hell? "No," said Staupitz. Bear the attack, for "God will use you as his instrument to accomplish great things." But how can I love a God who keeps men confused and uncertain whether or not he has chosen them for salvation, asked Martin. If you must speculate about the mystery of predestination, advised Staupitz, "look at it through the wounds of Christ." That is, hold to what Christ reveals about God; don't lose your balance prying into exalted questions which God has not meant us to understand. Staupitz really meant: This is the way to be humble and worthy enough to merit God's favor. But the advice helped Martin anyway, although it took him a while to realize this fact.

Best of all, as Luther gratefully confessed in a letter of 1518, Staupitz helped him to understand repentance. The chief theologians whom Martin had studied taught an elaborate technique of private confession, training men to ransack their memory for every hidden sin and to promise detailed penances or works as the proof of their repentance. Some theologians also had taught that it makes little difference with what motive a person comes to confession; even the base motive of fearing punishment will suffice, for the grace of the Sacrament of Penance will bring him around to the love of God. Staupitz, on the contrary, showed Luther that real repentance is not an elaborate technique; it is simply and unaffectedly casting oneself upon God's mercy. Moreover, this repentance begins in your love of God; it is not a way to win God's love.

"Your words pierced me like the arrows of the mighty," wrote Luther, and examining Scripture again he realized that the vicar was right. So "while formerly hardly a word in all of Scripture had been more bitter to me than 'penitence'—although I carefully simulated it, even before God, trying to express an assumed and forced love,—now no word sounds sweeter or more pleasant to me." Shortly thereafter, through the study of biblical languages, he came to realize that the Latin translation of Jesus' word in Matthew 4:17 was partly responsible for the common misinterpretation. The Latin Bible read, "Do penance, for the kingdom of heaven is at hand." *Penitentia* meant both the attitude in the heart and the works of penance, but it is easy to see where the emphasis had been laid. Luther now saw that the translation should be "repent," for the Greek original clearly means "be transformed in your mind."

"If Dr. Staupitz, or rather God through Dr. Staupitz, had not helped me out of these attacks, I should have been swallowed up by them and plunged into hell long ago," Luther confessed. After the Reformation burst out, Staupitz remained within the Roman Catholic church, but the two remained friends, and years later, as Staupitz neared death, the reformer wrote in a tender letter to him: "Through you the light of the gospel first began to shine out of the darkness into my heart."

Do all these violent emotions seem terribly overdone? Yes, surely, to any person whose emotions are limited to a narrow range. Yes, to someone who considers religion mere imagination anyway. Yes, to someone for whom the old church's prescriptions automatically settle all personal problems. Yes, perhaps, for various other reasons. But keep some other points in mind. Just now you are merely reading about these events; for Martin Luther the issues became a matter on which he would stake his life. Moreover we have the advantage of over 450 years' hindsight; he had to grope and fight his way through a wilderness. In some ways the difference is as great as a family holiday drive today from the midwestern plains to the Pacific coast on superhighways is from the Lewis and Clark expedition to the West in 1804–06.

Breakthrough

Meanwhile the young professor continued to lecture on the Psalms. The light of a new understanding of a merciful God was beginning to dawn. But Dr. Luther was not free from his entanglement yet.

The haunting view of the just and terrible Judge still held him captive. Luther had made important progress in his theology. He had learned to concentrate on the really central problem of man: sin and forgiveness—that is, life in the presence of God. He had reached the conviction that Scripture must be the supreme norm of our understanding of God and man, and that Christ is the master key to Scripture from beginning to end. He knew that the gospel is "the power of God for salvation," the good news that God is merciful as well as strictly just.

But exactly here Luther came up against a stone wall. In the gospel "the righteousness of God is revealed through faith for faith; as it is written, 'The righteous shall live by faith' [Romans 1:17]." Luther already knew that God's righteousness is revealed in the law, which shows sinners how far they fall short of his justice. But how can one trust in a merciful God if the gospel also reveals the same stern, righteous God?

The battle continued between the man and the Book. Suddenly the light streamed in. Luther described the event much later:

"I had been seized with a terrific eagerness to understand St. Paul in the Epistle to the Romans. A single expression in chapter one stood in the way: 'the righteousness of God.' I hated that word, which I had been taught to understand as the righteousness with which God is righteous, and punishes unrighteous sinners. However blamelessly I lived as a monk, I felt that in God's presence I was a sinner with a most uneasy conscience, nor could I trust that he was appeased by my works of satisfaction. I did not love this righteous God who punished sinners. Indeed, I hated him and raged at him with a fierce and disturbed conscience. Nevertheless, I continued to knock impatiently at St. Paul's door, thirsting intensely to know what he meant in this passage.

"I meditated day and night. Finally, by the mercy of God, as I pondered the connection of the words, 'In it the righteousness of God is revealed, as it is written, The just shall live by faith,' I began to understand what the righteousness of God means. It is the righteousness by which a just man lives by the gift of God, namely, by faith—in other words, that by which a merciful God justifies us through faith. I felt that I was completely reborn, that I had entered through open gates into paradise itself. From then on the whole face of the scriptures was changed for me. As much as I had hated this word 'righteousness of God' before, now just as fondly I praised it as the sweetest word I knew, so that this verse in Paul became for me the gate of paradise. . . ."

We cannot be certain exactly when this event took place but probably it was in 1514, and we know that it was in the tower of the monastery at Wittenberg. Accordingly it has often been called "the Tower experience." This label is hardly accurate, for it was no emotional religious experience like the call of Paul or the conversion of John Wesley. A better designation would be "the Tower insight," for it consisted of a fresh understanding of what Scripture means by the gospel, a liberating awareness of the way God deals with men. I do not earn or bargain my way to God's approval; he gives it to me in sheer mercy. Faith is my acceptance of this gift. For faith is not simply an act of my mind, believing a religious statement to be true; it is the response of my whole being when God graciously offers to accept me as his child.

This rather simple insight—can it really have been so decisive? On the one hand Martin himself did not realize immediately all that it meant. On the other hand, this was not an event standing all alone. In retrospect Luther saw that his mind developed, not all of a sudden, but gradually during his writing and teaching career. Nevertheless the "Tower insight" may stand as a landmark as we trace Luther's life. It brought him out into the clear with the gospel in his hands. It made a new man out of Martin Luther, and that transformation led him, step by step, to reform the church.

PART THREE

The Showdown

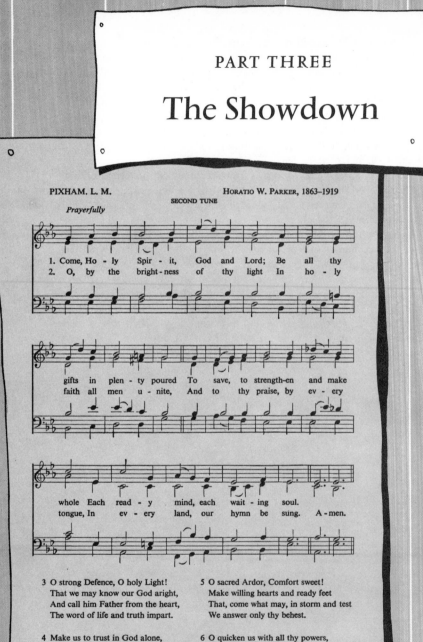

PIXHAM. L. M.

HORATIO W. PARKER, 1863–1919

SECOND TUNE

Prayerfully

1. Come, Ho - ly Spir - it, God and Lord; Be all thy
2. O, by the bright - ness of thy light In ho - ly

gifts in plen - ty poured To save, to strength-en and make
faith all men u - nite, And to thy praise, by ev - ery

whole Each read - y mind, each wait - ing soul.
tongue, In ev - ery land, our hymn be sung. A - men.

3 O strong Defence, O holy Light!
That we may know our God aright,
And call him Father from the heart,
The word of life and truth impart.

4 Make us to trust in God alone,
And Jesus for our Master own,
His yoke and teaching ne'er to change
For other doctrines new and strange.

5 O sacred Ardor, Comfort sweet!
Make willing hearts and ready feet
That, come what may, in storm and test
We answer only thy behest.

6 O quicken us with all thy powers,
Make strong our faith in weaker hours,
That, as good Christians in the strife,
We turn to thee in death and life. Amen.

Martin Luther, 1483–1546
Tr. Edward Traill Horn III, 1909–

14. The Pastoral Heart

THAT bare little room in the monastery tower—a less likely base of operations for storming the mighty papacy would be hard to imagine. "Enthusiastic papist" that he was at the time he discovered the gospel, Luther had not the slightest thought of challenging the old church system. As his theological insights gradually matured, however, he became increasingly sure that several things which he had been taught were far out of line with the gospel he found in Holy Scripture. It was a professor's business to challenge questionable theology and bring it into harmony with Scripture. Luther's bold efforts to do just this brought students flocking to hear him. What they heard, meanwhile, was more than a clever mind. So absorbed was the professor in guiding men's lives by the gospel of Christ that his hearers found themselves absorbing his earnest concern. His passion for truth was contagious.

Verbal Portrait

One student's memorandum (actually dating from a few years later) takes us into the very lecture room of Professor Luther. "He was a man of medium height, with a voice that combined sharpness and softness: it was soft in tone, sharp in enunciation. He spoke neither too quickly nor too slowly, but at a moderate pace, without hesitation, and very clearly, and in such beautiful order that everyone could see how the content of his exposition flowed out of the text itself. His lectures never contained anything that was not pithy and relevant. And as for the spirit of the man: if even the fiercest enemies of the gospel had been among his hearers, they would have confessed under the impact of what they heard, that they had witnessed no mere man but a spirit, for he could not have taught such amazing things from himself, but only from the influence of some good or evil spirit."

The young lecturer's method was not new. Most of his thoughts were culled from the common treasure of Christendom. Nevertheless his hearers found them not only spirited and refreshing, but also an unmistakable challenge to the currently fashionable theology. Through his lectures on the Psalms Luther grew measurably, both in his view of Christ as the key to all the Scriptures and the key to the

Christian life, and in his understanding of the way men become good and do good works.

Lectures on Romans

Luther's next lectures, on Paul's Epistle to the Romans, delivered between Easter, 1515, and September, 1516, were a work of genius. He was rapidly maturing, inwardly in his own faith and outwardly in his theology. He was more sure of himself. He had read more deeply in the works of the early church fathers, especially the best of them, Augustine. Deeper yet was his penetration into the Scriptures. It was here that he realized how radically sick contemporary theology had become. "I lost Christ in Scholastic Theology, but now I have found him again in Paul." Luther's teaching of repentance, forgiveness, faith, and the Christian life now took on sharper focus and more compelling power.

Probably the best summary of his course on Romans comes, not from his lecture room, but from a letter of pastoral counsel written during this same period to a fellow monk:

"Many men, not knowing the righteousness of God which is most abundantly and freely given us in Christ, seek to do good by their own powers, until they feel confident that they can stand before God adorned with their own virtues and merits. But this cannot possibly be done. You yourself used to hold this error. So did I, and even now I fight against it but have not yet conquered it. Therefore, my dear brother, learn Christ and him crucified. Despairing of yourself, learn to sing his praise: 'You, Lord Jesus, are my righteousness; I am your sin. You have taken on yourself what is mine, and given me what is yours.' Christ dwells only in sinners. This is why he came down from heaven. Ponder this love of his, and you will see how beautifully it will comfort and sustain you. For if by our own efforts and afflictions alone we can gain a quiet conscience, what did he die for?" The young teacher was asking troubling questions.

Theological Conflict

This fresh teaching brought Luther into sharp conflict with the theology then in vogue. All the major systems were grounded in the analytical philosophy of the ancient Greek, Aristotle. Most of them laid their emphasis, not on God's grace, but on all that man can do to make himself right with God. To a close friend Luther expressed his opinion of Biel, in whose thought he himself had been trained: "What he says is all very good—except when he speaks of grace, love, hope, faith, and goodness!"

However, Luther's teaching brought a powerful message to sensitive hearts. It was solidly backed by Scripture. One after another, Luther won his colleagues on the Wittenberg faculty over, until by the spring of 1517 he could say, "Our theology and St. Augustine are progressing very well. With God's help they rule at the university. Aristotle is gradually toppling from his throne. Indeed, no one can expect an audience if he does not lecture on the Bible or St. Augustine or some other eminent teacher of the church." Soon the theological curriculum itself would be revised to place the concentration on biblical studies. Luther had gained an able group of allies.

Other Duties

Meanwhile, if Luther's stature as a professor was growing, so were his duties outside the classroom. He had already been sub-prior of the Wittenberg monastery for two years. In 1514 he was chosen preacher of the town church. In May, 1515, the order elected him district vicar, overseer of eleven monasteries. Late in 1516 he wrote wryly to a friend:

"I need a couple of secretaries. All day long I do almost nothing but write letters. I am preacher at the monastery, and reader to the monks at mealtimes. I am asked to preach daily in the parish church, I am director of studies in the monastery, district vicar—thus eleven times prior, business manager of our fish pond at Leitzkau, mediator in the Hersberg dispute at the court in Torgau, lecturer on Paul, and I am revising my lectures on the Psalms for publication. I seldom have time to say the seven daily devotions properly or celebrate mass, to say nothing of my own struggles with the world, the flesh, and the devil. You see what a lazy fellow I am!"

Luther's horizon had greatly broadened. Now a devout soul and a scholarly mind alone would not be enough. With eleven monasteries and a parish church under his care, he also needed a pastoral heart. Luther showed that he had it. His letters reveal him offering wise counsel to individuals, settling disputes, administering gentle but firm discipline. Sermons to monks and to townsmen were addressed helpfully to the deep needs of men. Even his Romans lectures in the university, as we saw, disclose the same pastoral heart. Luther's horizon, moreover, now embraced public affairs. He spoke out against abuses in church and state, even if they involved his own ruler, since public injustices brought harm to the souls entrusted to God's appointed leaders.

Then early in 1517 came a jolt to the earnest pastor. Father Luther had been preaching that sinners must humble themselves before God, accept his chastening, and amend their lives. Now in the confessional, when he urged parishioners to express sorrow for their sins and promise a better life, some of them replied that their sins were already forgiven. When he assigned them works of piety in order to prove their repentance outwardly, they retorted that they didn't need to do them. In his face they flaunted their indulgences, letters of pardon issued by the church, to prove their point. Father Luther was shocked. He refused to absolve and restore them to Communion. Offended, they went back to Father John Tetzel, the indulgence preacher who had sold them the letters. Tetzel, an imposing and influential man, was furious. This was an insult to his employer, the Archbishop of Mainz, highest prelate in Germany. Besides, as everybody knew, Tetzel also had power to excommunicate anyone who interfered with his commission to proclaim the church's pardons.

15. The Question of Forgiveness

WITTENBERGERS who had walked twenty miles to find Tetzel saw a shrewd salesman in operation. His agents carefully prepared a town for his arrival. Then, at the town gate, with the papal bull (a formal decree) authorizing the indulgence borne before him on a velvet or cloth-of-gold cushion, he was met by all the priests and monks, town councilmen, schoolmasters and students, men, women, and girls carrying banners and candles and singing as they marched in procession to the town square. A red cross was set up, the pope's banner was displayed, and Tetzel preached a dramatic sermon on "hell." All the bells in town rang, and as the procession moved to the largest church, organs played. Now the cross and papal banner were set up in the middle of the church, and Tetzel preached on "purgatory." Later he preached a third sermon on "heaven."

"God and St. Peter call you!" roared Tetzel. "Consider the salvation of your soul. You are tossed about in a furious tempest amid the temptations and dangers of this world. Are you sure you can reach the haven of salvation? . . . Listen to the voices of your dear dead relatives and friends, beseeching you, 'Pity us, pity us! We are in dreadful pain. For one little coin you can release us.' Remember, you can release them, for

'As soon as the coin in the coffer rings,
The soul from purgatory springs.' "

Tetzel boasted that he had saved more souls with his indulgences than Peter with his preaching. He declared that with the help of an indulgence, the pope could grant a man forgiveness of even the worst imaginable sin, for example, violating the Blessed Virgin Mary. All the people, reported Frederick Myconius, a young man who had heard this preaching, were convinced that buying indulgences was the one sure way to eternal life. Tetzel's take, therefore, was enormous.

Indulgences

Actually indulgences were not really sold, only a "donation" was asked. Of course, the instructions given to Tetzel prescribed what contribution was expected. Bishops and princes or persons of higher rank should pay at least twenty-five gold gulden; well-to-do burghers with an income of five hundred gulden or more: six; persons of very humble station: one-half to one gulden. There were other rates in between. The penniless were to receive an indulgence free. Meanwhile confusion might well arise among the masses. For instance, when Myconius as a penniless youth begged a free indulgence "for the love of God," Tetzel firmly brushed him off; and once a nobleman's wife asked her father confessor why Tetzel had directed her to contribute one hundred gulden.

Then, too, the indulgences were not meant to be selfish and mercenary. Official instructions decreed that agents were to promote sincere piety among the people. The unselfish motive of releasing others from purgatory was carefully cultivated. Further, these particular contributions were to go for the rebuilding of St. Peter's Cathedral in Rome, just begun but lagging for lack of funds. How noble, the instructions suggested, to help protect the sacred bones of Peter and Paul from desecration by rain and hail. Of course, cynical complaints had also been heard for over a century that by such means Italians were merely sucking Germany dry.

Father Luther, however, was not so bothered over these points; the indulgence system must be basically sound or the church would not have established it. But what do indulgences actually grant? On this point the people were hopelessly confused. Many believed they brought full forgiveness of sin to the contributors. Not so, said the official teaching. The Sacrament of Penance, which provides grace to forgive serious sins, consists of three acts: remorse or "contrition in the heart," "confession by mouth" to the priest, and then "satisfaction [or penance] by works." Any serious sin incurs both "guilt" before God, and "punishment." If a Christian dies with any guilt unabsolved, he burns in hell forever; sacramental absolution erases guilt. But a sin offends God's creation and God's church. This damage must be repaired by punishment, either here or in purgatory; besides, the penitent needs to demonstrate his sincerity by outward deeds. An indulgence, strictly speaking, applies only to these "satisfactions," reducing or canceling the punishment after guilt has been absolved. Tetzel's instructions stated explicitly that an indulgence benefits the contributor only if he has first "felt contrite and confessed."

On the other hand the instructions announced that the first great benefit of this indulgence was "the full remission of all sins." Some indulgence bulls, indeed, explicitly offered pardon "from punishment and from guilt." Furthermore authorities were still not agreed exactly what jurisdiction the pope had over purgatory.

With this kind of murky teaching, it is no wonder that people became confused. Here lay Luther's complaint. Many things about the indulgence system were obscure and many other things were damaging to a real understanding of Christianity.

Behind the Scenes

At the time Luther did not know that there was high-level chicanery behind Tetzel's indulgence trade. The princely family of Brandenburg sought power and glory. Joachim of Brandenburg was one of the seven electors of the Holy Roman Empire. But his younger brother Albert held no important office. Late in 1513 Albert secured an appointment as both Archbishop of Magdeburg and Bishop of Halberstadt. There were some difficulties, since it was contrary to church law for an official to hold two posts at once. Besides, it was illegal for a man under twenty-four to become a bishop at all; Albert was only twenty-three.

The difficulties were solved with ease by liberal use of money. The papal court could grant a "dispensation" exempting anyone from almost any regulation, if it found sufficient spiritual reasons—and if the fee was right. Something over a thousand ducats enabled Pope Leo to see the reasonableness of appointing Albert to both positions.

But a still juicier plum was within reach. With proper handling Albert might also become Archbishop of Mainz. That meant primate of all Germany, elector, and chancellor of the empire. Joachim had the necessary influence at Rome. Early in 1514 the pope was persuaded that Albert was the best possible candidate for Mainz. For the dispensation, His Holiness asked twelve thousand ducats, a thousand for each of the twelve apostles. Albert's agent offered seven thousand, a thousand for each of the seven deadly sins. Leo finally accepted ten thousand along with the customary fees of 12,300. All told, Albert was now 34,000 ducats in debt for the three offices.

To pay the fees, Albert secured a loan from the biggest banking firm in Germany. How would he ever repay it? The pope graciously helped him out. For the benefit of St. Peter's, the faithful of Germany would be offered an unusually generous indulgence, beginning in 1515 and lasting eight years. Albert could keep half of the proceeds to enable him to retire his bank loan.

Some of the other half, by the way, undoubtedly did benefit St. Peter's. Most of it, however, probably went for the pope's entertainments. A man of luxury and culture, Leo X also thought big. "The papacy is ours, let us enjoy it," he is said to have remarked upon his election. Within his eight-year reign, he emptied three papal treasuries: his predecessor's, his own, and his successor's.

The deal between Rome, the bankers, and Albert was kept fairly well under cover. But front-page news, as far as the people were concerned, was the pope's generous granting of an indulgence, with its invitation to honor Peter and its offer of such magnificent spiritual benefits, all in one package.

Opposition

Theological misgivings, meanwhile, were aired by a number of scholars, including a couple of Luther's later enemies. Frederick, the elector of Saxony, expressed more practical opposition. He forbade the pardon-hucksters to enter his territory. Like other princes he disliked seeing huge sums of money drained out of the country. Furthermore Albert's indulgence competed with his own. Hardheaded, shrewd, pious Frederick, who had once made an expensive pilgrimage to the Holy Land, was trying to assemble in the castle at Wittenberg the most valuable collection of holy relics in Germany. A papal indulgence had been granted to everyone visiting them during their annual display on All Saints' Day, November 1.

A remarkable collection it was: a piece of the wise men's gold, a nail from the cross, a piece of bread from the Last Supper, a twig from Moses' burning bush, a tooth of St. Jerome, and so on and so on. When the artist Lucas Cranach in 1509 prepared an illustrated catalogue, it contained 5,005 items. Staupitz and other agents continued to negotiate for more. By visiting the collection, which numbered 17,443 items in 1517, a person could receive release from 127,799 years and 116 days in purgatory.

Luther's growing criticism of the archbishop's indulgence characteristically probed deeper than that of his prince and his fellow theologians. They were treating symptoms. Luther tried to get to the heart of the issue: What role should indulgences play in securing genuine forgiveness of sins and encouraging a Christian life? In July and again on October 31, 1516, before Tetzel brought his high-pressure salesmanship to Wittenberg, Luther had preached on the subject. In February, 1517, he preached still more outspokenly. Indulgences, he suggested ironically, now meant indulging a person when he sins; seriously, the sales were preventing men from finding Christ. Elector Frederick was irritated; after all, this challenge threatened his own indulgence. At least, however, Luther's criticism could not be called mercenary. Frederick's income from the Castle Church indulgence helped to pay the faculty salaries at Wittenberg.

Attacking the Problem

In October Luther finally saw a copy of Albert's instructions to the hawkers. This was too much. The festering boil, this indulgence question, had to be lanced. The proper way was to have the question openly debated by theologians. Following age-old custom, Luther carefully drew up a series of statements which he would offer to defend in debate—try them on for size—but this did not commit him personally to them.

It is hard to tell what kind of reaction he expected. Less than two months earlier he had widely distributed an invitation to debate some scorching criticisms of scholastic theology. Eagerly he waited for the firecracker to go off. It was a dud. Not a single person accepted the challenge—or even bothered to denounce it. It was a frustrating experience for a man on fire with truth.

About midday on October 31, 1517, the day before the annual display of Frederick's holy relics, Professor Luther walked with his attendant from the Augustinian monastery through the marketplace to the Castle Church. On the north door, which served as the university bulletin board, he posted his Ninety-Five Theses. It was a routine action; no one paid any particular attention. For Luther, however, it was a serious move: "I had first prostrated myself in prayer that God would be with me." Later generations have celebrated the event as the birth hour of the Reformation.

The Ninety-Five Theses

This young professor, not quite thirty-four years old, did not think he was attacking the church but, rather, trying to defend it from abuses. So reads the heading of the theses: "Out of love for the truth and the desire to bring it to light, the following propositions will be

debated at Wittenberg under the chairmanship of the Reverend Father Martin Luther."

As Luther later looked back on the event, he was grimly amused at how immature he was—though he also realized that he was blazing a trail alone. At first glance the theses appear almost a stammering jumble. But two insights at least are clear, as we see from his letter to Archbishop Albert. First, "I deplore the gross misunderstanding among the people which comes from these preachers." Second, "Works of piety and love are infinitely better than indulgences."

Actually the theses did not attack any Roman Catholic doctrine. Indulgences themselves were still valid. So was the authority of priests as well as the idea of purgatory. And yet a revolution was in the making. Luther had no sure direction, but his experience of God's grace was guiding him. Three insights, gradually developing, stood out in his Ninety-Five Theses.

First, the church needed to clarify its teaching about repentance. The first thesis rings out like a trumpet call. "Our Lord and Master Jesus Christ, in saying: 'Repent!' intended that the whole life of believers should be repentance." Eventually his insight would mature and challenge the whole Roman Catholic view of the removal of sins. Already Luther was teaching his pupils that the Christian should realize that he lives at every moment only by God's forgiveness. This forgiveness comes freely and fully to every repentant believer, quite apart from indulgences. True repentance, therefore, delivers us from our selfish self-love. It patiently accepts God's chastisement for our sins, rather than trying to evade it as indulgences encourage us to do. It produces outward discipline of the flesh. It demands an honest, rigorous self-discipline.

Second, the church needed to clarify its teaching about indulgences. The practice of purchasing indulgences encouraged men to dodge repentance, not to amend their lives and to practice Christian love. What are indulgences then? As far as Luther was concerned, they merely cancel punishments which the church has imposed. In other words, indulgences applied to human church discipline, not to God's eternal forgiveness of sins.

Third, the church needed to clarify its teaching about its own nature. Contrary to the opinion of many authorities, the church did not somehow control God's forgiveness; it only proclaimed it. Nor did the church control purgatory; it simply offered prayers for souls there. The church supported indulgences by the doctrine that Christ and the saints had won an infinite treasure of merits, and the church could draw upon it. Luther retorted that "the true treasure of the church is the holy gospel of the glory and grace of God," and this treasure was not doled out by churchmen.

These deeper insights now supplied the power for the blow against shameful abuses: Why must the faithful sheep be fleeced, even to build St. Peter's? If the pope can release souls from purgatory, why doesn't he empty the place? Luther ended with a solemn warning to the church which was offering cheap grace: "Away with those who say to the people of Christ, 'Peace, peace,' when there is no peace!"

By intention, therefore, Luther's theses were no revolt against the church, but an open request to clean up the practice of indulgences and to clear up the obscure theory supporting them. This was the gist of the polite but pointed letters which, along with copies of his theses, he dispatched to Archbishop Albert and the Bishop of Brandenburg on the same day, October 31. This done, he went about his business as usual.

16. The Silencers

THE results of his decisive action amazed Luther. "Within two weeks," reported Myconius, "these theses were circulating throughout all Germany, and in a month throughout Christendom, as if the angels themselves were serving as messengers to bring them to the attention of all men. It is unbelievable how much talk they caused." Soon translated from their original Latin into German, the theses reached the common man. Very few ordinary people were aware of John Huss' suggestions for reform a century earlier. The printing press made a tremendous change in publicizing ideas. Copyrights were yet unknown so printers all over Germany threw off German and Latin copies by the thousands, much to Luther's annoyance; he said he would have expressed himself more distinctly if he had known what would happen.

Reactions

Public response to the theses was volcanic and varied. The note Luther had sounded was greeted by a roar of approval from some. "Here is the man we've been waiting for," cried an old Franciscan prior; immediately he wrote to Luther, "Go to it! You are on the right path!"

From the howls of others, it was clear that the physician had touched a raw nerve. Indulgence sales were down eighty percent in Brandenburg. Tetzel thundered from his pulpit, lit fires to warn people what happens to heretics and roused the other members of the Order of Preachers (the Dominicans) to stir up a clamor against Luther. Soon the Dominicans were boasting that they would have Luther banned and burned within a few weeks. Some of Luther's fellow Augustinians begged him not to drag the order into disgrace. To Luther's embarrassment, meanwhile, Wittenberg students showed their enthusiastic support by burning eight hundred copies of Tetzel's counter-blast against him.

Your theses are not uncatholic, the Bishop of Brandenburg advised him, but they are indiscreet; better be patient and keep quiet for the time being.

The man most painfully stung by Luther's challenge, Archbishop Albert, simply requested Rome to start a legal process to silence the arrogant monk. Albert made no reply to Luther himself. "Little fires are easily quenched," agreed His Holiness the Pope and directed the general of the Augustinians to order Luther to recant.

Support

Now a crucial question: What position would Luther's prince take? Luther soon learned from his close friend, George Spalatin, the elector's chaplain, that Frederick would offer his powerful protection. Too wily to announce public approval of the young professor suspected of heresy, Frederick simply insisted that Luther should receive a full and fair hearing before any condemnation was carried out in his territory.

The German Augustinians were to hold a general convention at Heidelberg in April, 1518. Perhaps this touchy affair could be settled through regular channels of monastic discipline. True, a rumor was abroad that if Luther left Wittenberg, he might meet with foul play. But that did not deter him, nor did the 350-mile journey, even though he had to walk most of the way. The convention was a triumph for Luther. The order did not censure him. Instead, it gave him an invitation to present his theology in a debate.

Luther's performance was brilliant. Well developed by now was his talent for stating the difference between theological opinions in daringly sharp and stimulating fashion. Several young visitors were completely won over to Luther's views. One was the Dominican Martin Bucer who later became an important reformer in Germany and England. Another was John Brenz, a leader in reforming southern Germany. Bucer's report was ecstatic: "Our leading men argued against him with all their might, but all their wiles could not budge him an inch. His calmness in answering is remarkable, his patience in listening is incomparable, in his explanations you would recognize the acuteness of St. Paul. His answers, so brief, so wise, and drawn from the holy scriptures, easily made all his hearers his admirers."

Bucer exaggerated. But at least Luther had shown his power in a free and open discussion of his theology. He had gained widespread respect and several positive allies. The order simply asked him to publish the treatise he had begun, explaining his Ninety-Five Theses and warding off misinterpretations.

Challenge

Meanwhile the artillery barrage of Luther's opponents was already well under way. Some of these opponents were insignificant. Others were far more formidable.

The first of these to appear was a Dominican, Professor John Eck of the University of Ingolstadt. Three years younger than Luther, with whom he had recently formed a friendship, Eck was winning fame as a debater, and he was keenly ambitious. In March, 1518, he published a treatise sharply attacking Luther's views, and calling him "a fanatic Hussite, heretical, seditious, insolent and rash, muddled, ignorant, and a despiser of the pope." Within two months Luther sent back a penned retort: "You have your choice: I will remain your friend, if you wish, or I will gladly meet your attack." Eck made his choice: a lifelong career of relentlessly opposing Luther.

The next salvo came in May from the court of Rome, under pressure from the Dominicans. Assigned to examine this "suspicion of heresy" case, Silvester Prierias, the pope's censor of books and official theological adviser, prepared his verdict in three days: *A Dialog on Papal Authority*. Like many Roman Catholics, Prierias based his attack on the assumption that the pope is infallible in matters of faith and morals though Rome did not declare this view formally dogmatic until 1870. Whoever denies that the infallible church has a right to do what she actually does is a heretic. Therefore Luther is "a leper with a brain of brass and a nose of iron." Prierias' colleague, the "attorney general" of the papal court, accordingly summoned Luther to appear in Rome within sixty days to recant.

It took Luther two days to write an eighty-page retort to the papal expert. "Ridiculous as Tetzel was, he was more acute than you. You cite no scripture. You give no reasons." More significantly, Luther insisted that both pope and church council can err, and only Scripture is the final authority.

In August Luther's German enemies actually forged documents, making it appear that Luther had viciously attacked the papacy and the papal court. Luther quickly disowned the tracts, but too late; they had already made a deep impression on both the emperor and the officials in Rome.

Explanations

Through the summer Luther dealt with such attacks one after another. But he also tried to explain his position more constructively. Completing his long treatise explaining the Ninety-Five Theses, he sent copies to Staupitz, the Bishop of Brandenburg, and Pope Leo. To the pope, whom he believed innocent of the uproar against him, Luther wrote: "I understand, Most Blessed Father, that certain persons have made my name loathsome to you, saying that I have tried to diminish the authority of the Supreme Pontiff, and therefore accusing me of being a heretic, an apostate, and a traitor. . . . Most Blessed Father, I cast myself at your feet. Raise me up or slay me, approve me or reprove me as you please. I shall recognize your words as the words of Christ speaking in you. If I have deserved death, I shall not refuse to die."

Luther's written explanations and other writings, meanwhile, show that he was increasingly loosening himself from the old patterns of the medieval church. Seeing the way his enemies were throwing threats around, he declared that there can be a false church as well as a true church. The Word of God must be distinguished from the words of men, even churchmen. The church of Christ certainly needed a reformation deep within, but the court of Rome was doing all it could to prevent it. Moreover the church of Rome has not always had the right to rule over all the other churches; that claim is just an historical development.

It exasperated Luther that his enemies would not show him from Scripture where he was wrong. The faculty of Mainz, whom Archbishop Albert consulted about Luther's theses, had simply replied, "We find that they restrict the power of the pope and the Apostolic See; on that point they contradict the opinions of many venerable doctors." This judgment seems about as far as his other adversaries cared to go—except to add personal slander. It proved sufficiently that Luther was guilty of heresy.

They had picked on the wrong man, however, if they thought that Luther would be abashed by libels or intimated by labels of "false" or "erroneous" or "heretical." He wrote to a good friend, "The more they threaten the bolder I am. He who is poor fears nothing, for he has nothing to lose." He was not simply being arrogant. He was convinced that what he was defending was the teaching of Christ. His teaching he was willing to leave in God's hands.

Would you think that these attacks now occupied all his time and energy? Far from it. Between October, 1517, and the fall of 1518 he issued almost a dozen simple treatises on the Christian life for the common people, such as an explanation of the Ten Commandments, another on worthy preparation to receive the Lord's Supper. He had other things on his mind, too, like the new program of studies at the university and the arrival in August of the brilliant young professor of Greek, Philipp Melanchthon.

Luther had discovered a phenomenal skill as a pamphleteer—the first man in history to recognize the vast potential of the printing press for reaching the public on crucial issues. His cause, indeed, concerned all people, not just scholars and church executives. For this reason, a fantastic number of his writings were sold. His works dominated the annual book fair at Frankfurt. By October, 1518, a printer far away in Basel, Switzerland, issued a volume of Luther's collected writings.

A Visit to the Cardinal

Meanwhile those who would silence Luther were tightening the noose. Pope Leo's advisers had decided that Luther was no longer merely suspected of heresy but actually a "notorious heretic." In August, therefore, the pope ordered Cardinal Cajetan, his legate (official representative) at the German imperial diet: "Compel the said Martin to appear before you. When you have him in your power, keep him under guard until you hear further from us." If Martin recanted, Cajetan could absolve him and restore him to the holy mother church. If he resisted, Cajetan was to ban not only Luther but all who followed or protected him. A similar letter went to Elector Frederick: "A certain son of iniquity, Friar Martin Luther, sinfully puffs himself up in the church of God, and apparently relying on your protection, fears the authority or rebuke of no one." Frederick was told that he should not sully the good name of his family, but deliver Martin to the cardinal.

What should Luther do: recant, stall for more time, go into hiding, try to make the elector assume responsibility, try to stir up a popular revolt? Luther's decision was clear. He would meet the cardinal at Augsburg. He realized that only the elector's aid would save him from imprisonment. On the other hand, he did not want the elector placed in an awkward position. Actually the elector was already a step ahead of him. Frederick "the Wise," a staunch German, and proud of his professor and his university, was quite aware of the political power he held. Partly because Frederick insisted that Luther be tried on German soil, the pope changed the summons from Rome to Augsburg. Frederick also took care to secure a safe-conduct from the emperor for Dr. Martin.

While Luther awaited the safe-conduct, Cajetan's aide visited him several times. First the aide used the gentle approach: If Luther would only recant, everything would be all right. But Luther had no intention of recanting what had not been proved wrong. Then the aide tried taunts. "Do you think Prince Frederick would take arms to protect you?" "I hope not." "Then where will you live?" "Under heaven," Luther answered. The Italian made a gesture of contempt.

Luther faced another walk of nearly three hundred miles. He had never been in greater danger. More than once he said to himself, "Now you are doing to die. What a disgrace you are to your parents." He reached Augsburg, footsore and ill.

On October 12, with proper etiquette, Luther prostrated himself before the cardinal. He said he had come to be instructed and would submit to the church's judgment. The cardinal, a Dominican of learning and integrity, assumed a fatherly attitude. He had received recent orders not to argue over Luther's theology. But when Luther asked where he erred, the learned theologian could not refrain from instructing him. Soon the monk and the cardinal were locked in combative argument.

For three days, in the presence of Vicar Staupitz and then two of Frederick's lawyers, the wrangle continued. Cajetan insisted that the pope is above church councils, Scripture, and the entire church. Luther retorted that "the pope is not above, but under the Word of God," and that some papal laws have twisted Scripture. Finally, Cajetan loudly ordered him to leave his sight and not return unless he was ready to recant. Luther wrote to George Spalatin that night that he did not intend to recant a single syllable. In a letter home, telling of the proceedings, he remarked irritably that the cardinal was as well suited to judge the case as an ass to play the harp.

Next day Luther wrote to the cardinal, apologizing for having spoken irreverently. No answer. Rumor soon arose that both Luther and Staupitz were to be arrested. Luther wrote a second letter to Cajetan, stating that he intended to leave. Again no answer. Frederick's advisers became uneasy. The rumors became stronger, and suddenly, very early on October 20, Luther, half-dressed, was secretly packed off on a borrowed horse in a rather ridiculous flight through the night. Cajetan was enraged.

Safely back in Wittenberg, Luther published a spirited account of the proceedings at Augsburg to inform the general public of what had happened. Even before returning, he had written an *Appeal from the Pope Badly Informed to the Pope Better Informed.* The elector was dismayed.

On October 31, 1518, exactly one year from the posting of the Ninety-Five Theses, Luther found himself writing to Spalatin an explanation of what had happened at Augsburg. How incredibly different had been this thirty-fifth year of his life. But he had been ready for it.

17. The Question of Church Authority

LUTHER had now had a taste of power politics. He never did become fully at home in it, and only gradually did he learn how God works through the affairs of men to chasten or to restore, to rule and to overrule. At just about the time Luther was writing to Spalatin, international politics had reached an extremely touchy point. The Turks were advancing in eastern Europe. Both the pope and the emperor needed taxes to pay for a war to beat them back. The emperor therefore summoned an imperial diet to meet at Augsburg to consider the question of taxing Germany. The German princes, however, brought before the diet another list of "grievances" against the church: "German money, contrary to nature, flies over the Alps; the pastors given to us are shepherds only in name; they care for nothing but the sheep's fleece, and they fatten on the sins of the people. . . ." The aged Emperor Maximilian, nearing the end of his days, was anxious to conciliate the electors in order to win their support for his grandson Charles, whom he wanted to be elected as his successor— and Frederick held a balance of power in the diet.

Luther, however, was still in an extremely exposed position. In November the pope had officially defined the doctrine of indulgences, so the ground for continued opposition seemed cut off. Later in the same month, meanwhile, Luther had sent to the printer an "Appeal" for a general council—a move which former popes had already declared heresy.

Would Frederick dare to harbor the heretic any longer? One counselor reminded the elector of the fable of the sheep who, at the advice of the wolves, sent away the watchdogs; the powers in Rome would accuse us all of being heretics, he concluded. Should Luther flee to France? The idea was vetoed. Should he be hidden in a castle?

Luther prepared for sudden departure from Wittenberg, and held a farewell dinner with some colleagues on December 1. During the dinner a letter arrived from his good friend Spalatin commanding him to stay. Later in December Frederick wrote a courteous but firm letter to Cajetan saying that he would send Luther to Rome or banish him only after he had been convicted of heresy.

The Golden Rose

Luther was soon to encounter more politics. Charles von Miltitz, a Saxon nobleman and minor official at the papal court, was now sent to Germany. Pope Leo wrote to Frederick announcing his intention to bestow upon him one of the highest honors that could come to a ruler, the Golden Rose. In the same breath, of course, he urged Frederick to help root out of the Lord's field that "son of perdition," Martin Luther, to prevent this "scabby sheep" from further infecting the sheepfold.

Miltitz's delicate assignment was to secure Luther's arrest without alienating Frederick, whose support the emperor wanted. On his own, however, Miltitz decided to gamble for higher stakes: He would actually reconcile the German heretic and the Roman pontiff. What a mark that would be on his record. Not yet out of his twenties, endowed with very moderate intelligence but immoderate vanity, Miltitz was the kind of man who believed that a deal could always be put over if people were properly manipulated.

Miltitz dangled the Golden Rose before Frederick. Then, perhaps because he thought the Saxons would be pleased, he heaped humiliation upon John Tetzel. Treated by everyone as a scapegoat, Tetzel, the erstwhile indulgence seller, had dropped out of sight and had retired to a monastery in Leipzig, actually fearful for his life. Miltitz would make a public show of "butchering the black sheep." Also, in a sly way, he would hint to both Saxony and Rome that the other side was eager for a reconciliation.

The papal diplomat, however, soon sensed that Frederick was a prince who could be neither needled nor wheedled. Miltitz's abuse of the dying Tetzel only brought sympathy from Luther. Luther even wrote Tetzel a letter of comfort: "Cheer up. You didn't start this affair. The child had quite a different father." And yet something astounding was accomplished. After interviews with Miltitz in January, Luther agreed that he would be silent if his enemies also remained silent, that the pope should appoint a German archbishop or bishop to show him the errors which he should recant, that Luther would write something for the common people, demonstrating his reverence for the Roman Catholic church. Parting from Dr. Martin with a kiss and tears, the commissioner sent a glowing report to Pope Leo that the heretic was ready to recant. Late in March Leo wrote Luther to welcome back his "beloved son," directing him to come straight to Rome where he could make his recantation to "a kind and merciful father."

The Changing Tide

Actually no one was fooled more than Miltitz himself. Leo's understanding of reconciliation and Luther's were poles apart. The Saxon court mistrusted the slippery diplomat, and Luther was aware that Miltitz's farewell was a "Judas kiss and crocodile tears." Anyway, other events were already changing the tide, leaving Miltitz's schemes high and dry.

Old Emperor Maximilian died on January 12, 1519. Leading candidates to succeed him were Francis, the young king of France, and Maximilian's nineteen-year-old grandson Charles, whose maternal grandparents were Ferdinand and Isabella of Spain. The pope was extremely concerned. At almost any cost he wanted to prevent the election of the Hapsburg Charles. Charles already had inherited control of Austria, the Low Countries, Spain, and Naples, and if he also became emperor of Germany, he would be too powerful. Francis of France suited the pope much better, but the king was unpopular in Germany. The pope could not persuade Frederick of Saxony to become a candidate. A last-minute offer from Orsini, the papal legate at the imperial election, however, outdid even Miltitz's wildest imagination: If Frederick would support Francis, the pope would offer the "red hat"—appointment as a cardinal—to anyone whom Frederick might select. What an irony if Frederick had accepted and appointed Luther. But he didn't. Charles had the election sewed up anyway, with his campaign expenses of nearly a million gold gulden. On June 28 the election took place, Charles won, and Leo had to make the best of it. Though his political plans were frustrated, the pope still meant to win all religious conflicts.

Soon Professor John Eck of Ingolstadt University stepped forth with a challenge to a public debate at Leipzig. Luther had ignored other attacks, but now he felt released from his promise of silence.

He had wanted his theology to be openly tested in the light of Scripture. A sharp debate would clear the air—one way or the other.

How you judge Eck depends on how you regard the church. Does the church never err? Was the way it historically developed automatically right? Then Eck deserves credit as one of the first to see clearly that Luther's program meant not reform but revolution, and he deserves credit as a consistent, persistent opponent of Luther's heresy. On the other hand, if the church lives only by venturesome faith and the forgiveness of God, if it sometimes becomes self-sufficient and even tyrannical and must constantly be restored, then Eck was an enemy of the reform of the church.

As an adversary of Luther, in any case, Eck was crafty. It was not Luther whom he publicly challenged, but Dr. Andreas Carlstadt, Martin's bumbling colleague. Yet Eck's published proposals for debate did not attack Carlstadt's theology; they zeroed in on Luther's recent statements about papal authority.

Luther, knowing that Eck wanted to get at him, busily studied Scripture, church history, and canon law, digesting an amazing amount of material in a few months. The real church, he was coming to think, did not depend on the Roman Catholic organization. In March he wrote to Spalatin, "Eck is already boasting as if he had won a contest in the Olympics. I am studying the papal decretals for my debate. I whisper this in your ear: I do not know whether the pope is Antichrist or his apostle, so terribly do his decretals corrupt and crucify Christ, that is, the truth." This was an ominous thought. According to the Book of Revelation, Antichrist, the embodiment of all evil, would try to seize power from God himself. Often during the Middle Ages prophets of woe had predicted his coming, and extremists had connected him with the pope. Were they really right?

The Debates

Late in June two wagonloads of Wittenbergers rode into Leipzig. Two hundred students accompanied them, armed with spears and other weapons, for it was known that the Leipzigers were hostile. Religious processions, services, formal speeches, wrangling over rules, the packed throng in the hall of Duke George's castle, student brawls outside, all these gave the debate more excitement than a Rose Bowl game. But more was at stake than a game. For a week Eck and Carlstadt argued. Eck clearly had the edge.

Finally, on July 4, Luther mounted the speaker's stand opposite Eck's, and for five days the two greatest debaters in Germany bombarded each other over the supremacy of the pope. An eyewitness described the pair: "Martin is of medium height, so worn out from study and care that you can almost count his bones. . . . He is wonderfully learned in the Bible, and has almost all its texts at his fingertips. He knows Greek and Hebrew well enough to evaluate the translations. He speaks fluently, with an immense stock of ideas and words at his command. In manner he is courteous and friendly, not at all stern or arrogant; good-humored in company, lively and poised, cheerful-looking no matter how hard his enemies press him. What most men chide in him is that his answers are too rash and cutting. . . . Eck is a tall, heavy, square-set fellow with a full voice and strong lungs. He would make an actor or town crier, but his voice is rather rough than clear. His eyes and mouth and whole face remind you more of a butcher or soldier than a theologian. He has a fine memory; if only his understanding equaled it! He shoots out an immense volley of thoughts without any order, many of them inept, and thus he deceives his audience. With astonishing craft he switches the debate from one subject to another, and sometimes imputes his own absurdities to his opponent." Observers judged that Eck was Luther's superior in medieval theology; the two were about equal in canon law; Luther had the edge in early church history, and a vast advantage in scriptural knowledge.

Was the topic Luther and Eck debated important? Duke George's remark may have our sympathy: "What does it matter whether he is pope by divine right or by human right? He's still the pope!" But the question was crucial, nonetheless. Any criticism of the Roman Catholic system was automatically heresy if Christ had made the bishop of Rome the infallible ruler over all the churches "by divine right." That Christ had actually done so, Eck tried to prove from Matthew 16:18, "You are Peter, and on this rock I will build my church," saying that as Peter's successor, the pope is the head of the church on earth. No, said Luther, the "rock" on which Christ founded his churh is not Peter as a person, but the sturdy faith which Peter confessed. The church of Christ is not the Roman Catholic ecclesiastical machine; it is Christ's believers who proclaim the Word and administer the sacraments as he commanded. Christ himself is not absent from us in heaven; he is with us, the head of the church even on earth. He is infallible; his believers are not. Church leaders and even church councils can make mistakes.

ECK: Luther is setting himself above popes and councils.

LUTHER: No, I am setting Scripture there.

The bombshell burst when Eck declared: "You are defending the views of Huss!" That was a nasty charge to Leipzigers; they had suffered much from the Hussite rebellion. A century before, John Huss of Bohemia had been burned at the stake for teaching that Christ was the head of the church rather than the pope, that the Bible is the Christian's guide. Following Huss' martyrdom, his countrymen rose in bloody revolt. Luther retorted that he did not approve of the Hussite heresy. But as an afterthought he remarked that not all of John Huss' views were heretical; in fact, some were perfectly Christian. Said one eyewitness: "These words fell like a stone upon the hall. 'Plague take him!' shouted Duke George so loudly that the whole audience could hear him, as he put his arms akimbo and wagged his head." From then on Eck tarred Luther with the Bohemian brush at every opportunity, charging Luther as the "patron of the Hussites," though Luther vigorously protested the insinuation. Eck had scored a big point. He meant to damn Luther now as a subversive heretic.

After five days on the subject of church authority, the following five on purgatory, indulgences, and penance were an anticlimax. The debate dragged to a close on July 14. The parting shots between the two revealed their stalemate.

LUTHER: "The reverend doctor penetrates the scriptures as deeply as a water spider the water; indeed, he flees from them as the devil from the cross. With all reverence to the church fathers, I prefer the authority of scripture."

ECK: "The impatient monk sets himself up as an oracle who alone understands scripture, better than any of the fathers."

18. Charters of a Reformation

WHO had won the Leipzig debate? Eck, to be sure, said he did. He had routed the "monsters" from Wittenberg and had "roused the people to disgust for Luther's errors." Without waiting for the verdict from the official judges, the theological faculties of Erfurt and Paris, Eck toured around Germany and then went down to Rome to receive applause and prepare the ground for Luther's final downfall.

Divided Opinion

Some people, meanwhile, judged the debate quite differently. New students flocked to Wittenberg. Parts of Germany were distinctly cool to Eck. A humanist published a clever satire against him, *The Planed-Down Eck,* its title punning on his name, which means "corner" in German. The pompous doctor became the laughingstock of Germany. Significantly, too, the official judges found the debate such a hot potato that Erfurt never did return a verdict, and Paris —supposedly the leading school in Christendom—could not make up its mind for almost two years.

Almost everybody was taking sides. The showdown was coming. Influential humanists wanted freedom of learning for scholars and a simple, edifying Christianity for all Europe. They had recently rallied behind John Reuchlin, the scholar of Hebrew literature, when crabbed inquisitors and scholastics had persecuted him. They had kept up a running fire of satire against complexity and superstition and corruption in the Christian church. Now many of the humanists greeted Luther as another liberator, "a Daniel sent by Christ to correct abuses and restore the teaching of the gospel." Outstanding among them were the young scholar Philipp Melanchthon, and the artist Albrecht Dürer, who spoke of Luther as "the Christian who has helped me out of great anguish."

The great humanist, scholar, and author Erasmus, however, remained neutral. He pointed out that if men would promote sound learning and the peace of Europe, then through a good educational program, church and state might teach all men "a life worthy of Christ." But Erasmus saw with grief that Luther's policy was leading to "tumult." He had no love for Luther's enemies, but neither would he commit himself to a person who, he feared, lacked moderation.

Far more consistently, the German nationalists lined up on Luther's side. Long had they waited for a leader who would risk everything "for the glory of the fatherland and its freedom from the Roman tyrants." Especially the petty knights dreamed patriotically of a free and united Germany. Their fiery young spokesman, Ulrich von Hutten, a well-born humanist poet, volunteered to join their cause to this "German Hercules" who would slay the many-headed Roman beast. Through tracts, poems, woodcut posters, and personal action, this militant pressure group sought to rouse all Germans for the coming fight. They prepared for war and offered Luther their armed protection. Should he make use of it?

These were exciting times and perplexing choices to face. From the southwest corner of Germany a law professor wrote: "All of Switzerland, Constance, Augsburg, and a good part of Germany cling to Luther. Much in him you would praise and defend; but again there are some things which seem a bit too strong. There are blemishes in the Lutheran teachings which I dislike." From Constance, a future Catholic bishop: "Take for example his tract on Confession, which every old woman in the street knows. What Luther says is surely very true, but it is not wise to set such difficult matters before the whole world." A professor in what is now Belgium: "That stupid ass (another prominent theologian) constantly bawls against Luther, and only succeeds in getting all the people to buy Luther's books, thinking that there must be some good in them if they so displease the cheese-eater." Cartoons and doggerel rhymes taking either side of the argument were placarded for the common people in town and village. One faction would put the posters up, another would rip them down. Somebody was likely to get hurt in the process. Name-calling eventually leads to blows.

"The Roman Sodom"

For Luther, meanwhile, the Leipzig debate had indeed cleared the air. Until this time he had behaved as an accused man willingly awaiting a fair trial. Henceforth he assumed a fearful responsibility. In the name of God, "the Roman Sodom" also would be summoned to trial, and if she would not be reformed, she would be forsaken. Early in 1520 he discovered that many of the papal laws were actually based on forged documents; in John Huss' writings he found many thoughts which were truly evangelical. More than ever he felt that God's judgment was near.

This wrathful attitude he did not assume lightly. Again and again he was haunted by the question, "Are you alone the Holy Spirit's nest egg in these last days? Could God have let his people remain in error all these years?" His reassurance came through the Word. "Oh, with what great effort, even though I had scripture on my side, did I labor to justify my own conscience, when I faced the responsibility that I alone should rise up against the pope and treat him as the Antichrist. How often did my heart pound and accuse me: 'Are you alone wise? Are you sure that all others are in error? What if you are the mistaken one, and are leading many people astray so that they will all be eternally damned?' This lasted until Christ with his own sure Word strengthened me, so that my heart stopped pounding and became like a cliff on the seashore which laughs at the waves of the pope's arguments that dash against it." Lead people astray? More dangerous to souls would be "wicked silence."

A Flood of Writings

Armed with this Word, Luther set to work with almost super-human energy to proclaim his message, dashing off books and tracts faster than three presses could print them. Since printing was inexpensive and Luther took not a penny for his writing, his "paperback" tracts could be sold very cheaply. Most important of all, his emphasis on the gospel was getting through to the common people. A young chaplain far away in Basel introduced himself to Luther thus: "I see that your teachings are of God, my dear friend. Daily they are winning many souls for Christ, leading them from wickedness to true Christian piety."

As far as the public was concerned, four of Luther's treatises stood head and shoulders above all the others. So important do they remain for understanding Luther that to this day they are known as his Reformation Manifestos. Written in 1520, during the tense days when all Germany was waiting for the pope's bull excommunicating Luther, they reveal the masterful clarity with which Luther realized what he was to do. They were charters of the church's reformation. Now Luther was ready for his twofold task, to clear the ground and to rebuild the church of his day.

Treatise on Good Works

The *Treatise on Good Works,* published in June, dealt constructively with the foundations of Christian living. It was frankly addressed to laymen. As Luther said in his dedicatory letter to Duke John, Frederick's younger brother: "Would to God that in my whole life, with whatever ability is mine, I had helped one layman to be better. I would be satisfied to let all my other books perish." Opponents had often charged—and still do—that Luther's teaching of "salvation through faith alone" led to moral irresponsibility. Here Luther faced this challenge. "When I exalt faith and reject works done without faith, they accuse me of forbidding good works. Actually, I am trying hard to teach the genuine good works of faith."

Luther's magnificent explanation of the Ten Commandments expands this. Faith is not one work or virtue beside the others; it is the source from which alone come all truly good works. Faith is not pious talk of religious routine; it is "to trust God with the heart and look to him for all good. This faith, faithfulness, confidence deep in the heart, is the true fulfilling of the First Commandment," that is, to have no other gods. Morality is not mere outward action, but doing right because we want to do right.

Walls of Straw

On this religious foundation was built his next great treatise, *An Address to the Christian Nobility of the German Nation, Concerning the Reform of Christian Society* (August, 1520), which for sheer influence upon public affairs surpassed all of his other works. Into it were gathered the grievances of centuries, expressed and mute, over "the misery and distress of suffering Christendom." But what made this appeal so different and so effective was its timing and its constructive religious focus. The situation in Germany was tense; excited and confused people were looking for an answer. Luther provided a sense of direction, a plan of procedure, even a prospect of stability and new hope. Here sounded the voice of a leader.

Luther probed straight to the heart of Christendom's trouble. "The Romanists, with great adroitness, have built three walls about them, behind which they have defended themselves until now in such a way that no one has been able to reform them. This has been the cause of terrible corruption throughout all Christendom." His description of the walls was powerful. First, when civil authorities try to curb abuses in the church, the churchmen claim that "the spiritual power is above the civil power." Second, when anyone attempts to criticize them out of Scripture, churchmen object that the interpretation of Scripture belongs to no one but the pope. Third, if threatened with a church council, they reply, "No one can call a council but the pope."

These walls, retorted Luther, are "mere straw and paper"; let us blow them down! Is the "spiritual estate" (class) above the "civil estate"? Nonsense! "All Christians are truly of the 'spiritual estate.' Baptism, gospel, and faith alone make us a spiritual and Christian people." Hence, "through baptism all of us are consecrated to the priesthood." As 1 Peter 2:9 says, "You are a chosen race, a royal priesthood. . . ." Here, challenging the whole medieval conception of the priesthood, is Luther's first bold announcement of the Protestant principle of the priesthood of all believers. What it really means will become clearer as we proceed; it does not mean that the clergy is abolished, nor that a person comes to Christ strictly on his own, in any way he pleases. But if all Christians are equal heirs of Christ, then the ordained minister is not a man elevated into a privileged caste, but an officeholder. Through the will of the community of believers, he is chosen from among his equals and charged to wield a certain authority for the others. That authority is simply a ministry or service: the administration of the Word of God and the sacraments.

The second wall—that the interpretation of Scripture belongs to no one but the pope—is "still more flimsy and worthless." Popes err. It cannot be proved that they alone may interpret Scripture. Similarly, the third wall—that only the pope can call a council— "falls of itself." Then who shall reform this usurped church? Suppose the clergy will not call a council to do the job. In such an emergency, who else should take the lead but those Christians who already bear public responsibility, the civil authorities? As "leading members of the church," princes and town councils must help the gospel to be rightly taught throughout Christendom, and help see to it that the church shall be the church. The church's constitution and teaching are not entrusted to the clergy alone.

A real church council, Luther then continued in the second part of his treatise, could drastically overhaul the church, ridding it of its abominable greed, worldliness, and tyranny. With his specific suggestions, few of them new, thousands of Christians would wholeheartedly agree.

Part three of the treatise went still further, with twenty-seven sections of proposals for reforms in church and civil society which might be undertaken, on a large or small scale, either by civil authorities or by a great church council. Once again, papal pretensions and abuses were lashed. "Compare the two—Christ and the pope," Luther summed up. "Christ washed his disciples' feet, the pope as a great favor allows people to kiss his feet." Suggestions for reforms in church practice followed, and including such things as reform of monastic orders, the regulation of worship and pilgrimages, and marriage of the clergy. Many rules and restrictions of the church, he declared, were manifestly unfair. Therefore "if something is opposed to God, and harmful to man in body and soul, then any community, city council or government not only has the right to put a stop to it, without the will or knowledge of pope or bishop, but they are bound on their souls' salvation to prevent it, even against the will of pope and bishop, though these ought to be the first to forbid it." The suggestions continued, covering educational needs from common schools to universities, and various social, economic and political reforms that were needed.

"I have pitched my song in a high key," concluded Luther. He had laid out a bold platform for positive action; if others could improve on it, so much the better. "God give us all a Christian mind, and especially to the Christian nobility of the German nation true spiritual courage to do the best that can be done for the poor church."

The Church's Captivity

Scarcely had Germany recovered from the impact of Luther's bold appeal when he published *The Babylonian Captivity of the Church* (October, 1520). According to Luther, as the Jews had once been carried off into slavery, so the true sacraments have been "subjected to a miserable captivity by the Roman court, and the church has been robbed of all her liberty."

Luther maintained that the number of the sacraments should not be seven but two: Baptism and the Lord's Supper. God comes to us in many ways, but the name of "sacrament" ought to be restricted to those rites in which Christ himself has attached a definite promise of grace to a definite material sign—the water in Baptism, the bread and wine in the Supper. On this basis several of the Roman Catholic rites, though solemn ceremonies, do not qualify as sacraments.

Further, Luther took a fresh look at the use and meaning of the sacraments. They are not injections of grace, automatically effective. They are gifts from God containing a divine promise, intended to nourish and exercise faith. "These two—the promise and faith—must go together. Without the promise there is nothing to believe; without faith the promise remains without effect." Faith, then, is a firsthand thing. "Can I believe for another, or make another believe? Where there is a divine promise, everyone must stand on his own feet, everyone will give an account for himself. By the same token, no one can commune for any other." Luther wanted to emphasize that religion was an intensely personal matter, rather than an affair of churchly routines and regulations.

This leads us to Luther's attack upon the priestly system which had brought Christendom into this captivity. In the medieval view of ordination he found "the roots of that detestable tyranny of the clergy over the laity"—the "first wall" of Roman Catholicism. Through the all-encompassing network of sacraments, Rome had dominated men's lives while it corrupted Christ's true sacraments. Luther therefore proceeded to examine the "seven" sacraments, one after another. For example, who gave Rome the right to withhold the cup from the laity in the Lord's Supper? Who gave her the right to dictate that in the sacrament bread and wine change miraculously into Christ's body and blood? Who gave her the right to turn God's free gift of the Supper into a human work, a sacrifice offered back to God in order to claim a reward from him?

For many, reading this treatise was a shattering experience. If man can be saved from everlasting death only by God's grace through the sacraments, and if these sacraments are to be had only through the church of Rome, then *The Babylonian Captivity* struck at the very heart of religion, and of society as well. The emperor's confessor declared that the treatise shocked him from head to foot. Erasmus, who had hoped that the bold Wittenberg movement could be kept peacefully within the church, exclaimed, "The breach is beyond repair." He and many other moderates now drew back to the bosom of the old church. Young King Henry VIII of England wrote a lengthy theological book to refute Luther, earning from the pope the august title, "Defender of the Faith." On the other hand, the treatise completely won over to Luther's side a number of thoughtful men, including John Bugenhagen, who later became one of the most effective of Lutheran reformers.

Christian Freedom

One month later appeared a little tract so astonishingly different from the previous two that we can scarcely believe it was written by the same man. This was *The Freedom of a Christian*. Probably the most beautiful treatise that Luther ever wrote, it betrays not the slightest breath of the controversy in which he was embroiled.

The papal bull threatening excommunication for Luther was already published. Miltitz, however, made a last-ditch effort at conciliation. He persuaded Luther to write Pope Leo, assuring him that his attack on the papacy was not intended personally. That was the truth; but how Luther expressed it in his letter to Leo without sounding apologetic is a fairly remarkable achievement. He counseled the pope on the dangers of papal corruption. Along with the letter Luther enclosed a copy of *The Freedom of a Christian*.

The tract, which soon spread widely among the common people, was never described better than by Luther's own words: "It is a small book if you regard its size. Unless I am mistaken, however, it contains the whole of Christian living in a brief form, if you grasp its meaning." As in the treatise on good works, Luther once more addressed the simple man.

What is the freedom which a Christian has? Is it different from that which the non-Christian looks for? Luther sets down the theme of his tract in two striking sentences: "A Christian is a perfectly free lord of all, subject to no man. A Christian is a perfectly dutiful servant of all men, subject to all." Paul had said the same thing: "Though I am free from all men, I have made myself a slave to all" (1 Corinthians 9:19); "Owe no one anything, except to love one another" (Romans 13:8). Luther's first sentence describes faith in Christ, which makes a man free and in a sense the equal of any man. The second describes the love which faith begets, which leads a man freely to serve others.

Faith is the "wedding ring" which unites us with Christ, so that what he has done for us becomes effective in us. This is the power that makes us cheerfully obedient to God, and frees us from our selfishness and our uneasy, grudging rivalry with others. Faith therefore makes us "kings and priests in Christ." I am free as a king; even evil and suffering serve me. But faith also makes us concerned, responsible to "pray for others and teach one another the things of God."

Faith is "working through love," as Paul said (Galatians 5:6). Love is the power which cheerfully serves our neighbors. May a Christian never look out for himself? Of course, but he cares for himself not out of selfishness, but in order to help others more effectively; this, indeed, is the incentive for a Christian to discipline himself, to do his best. "I will give myself as a Christ to my neighbor, just as Christ offered himself to me." In short, a Christian "lives in Christ through faith, and in his neighbor through love."

19. The Showdown

LUTHER's great treatises clearly issued from a heart that had already wrestled through the problem of attaining peace with God. The treatises also indicated that his first and most passionate concern was for the welfare of the one true church of Christ; his intention was constructive, not destructive. If Luther was a rebel, he was rebelling as a loyal son of the church. Rome, of course, did not and could not see the matter that way. To Leo, Luther was a limb of Satan, an arrogant monk standing only on his own private opinions.

Condemnation

Finally Rome was ready to act. A committee of cardinals, aided by Eck, drew up the bull *Exsurge Domine,* which condemned forty-one teachings of Luther as "heretical, or scandalous, or false, or offensive to pious ears, or misleading to simple minds, or opposed to catholic truth, respectively." It ordered Luther to recant within sixty days or be officially judged a heretic. On June 15, 1520, at his hunting lodge outside Rome, Leo signed the bull with its eloquent introduction, "Arise, O Lord, and judge thy cause. A wild boar has invaded thy vineyard. . . ."

The condemnation had to be pronounced. What it would accomplish, however, was another question. Indeed, how to get the bull announced in Germany so that the sixty-day period of grace could start running proved a fantastically difficult question. Eck, who accepted the task of publishing it, could vouch for that. Local edicts denounced Luther. His books were burned and he himself was burned in effigy. But so violently had public opinion swung to Luther's side that some princes and magistrates forbade the public posting of the papal bull, and sometimes copies were torn down as soon as they were put up. Eck was snubbed and lampooned in posters. In Duke George's Leipzig, rioters threw Eck's servants out of an upper window. Young Ulrich von Hutten urged his fellow Germans on to freedom, pressed the knights to prepare for war, and called on Luther to remain steadfast.

The young Emperor Charles, who might have been able to ease the tension, was determined to uphold and carry out Rome's judgment. He had already ordered Luther's books burned in his inherited lands. Men everywhere predicted darkly that Germany would be drenched in blood. Erasmus deplored the unreasonableness of both sides.

Amid all the excitement, the two calmest people seemed to be Elector Frederick and Luther. The elector simply continued to insist upon fair play, arguing that Luther's views had not received a free hearing. Luther, besides issuing the treatises we have noted, continued lecturing, preaching twice daily, and writing devotional works. He warned that an effort to crush him might raise up many other men in protest. As for Hutten's preparation for war, Luther declared firmly: "I am unwilling to fight for the gospel with force and slaughter. The world is overcome by the Word." Meanwhile he appealed to the emperor: "I do not want to be protected if I am found ungodly or a heretic. I ask for only one thing: that neither truth nor falsehood be condemned without being heard and defeated."

Bonfire

Finally, on October 10, the papal bull reached Luther. The sixty days now began to run out. Luther, however, continued his activities. First he dashed off a tract, *Against the Damnable Bull of Antichrist.*

Then, very early on the morning on December 10, Philipp Melanchthon posted a grim notice on the university bulletin board, the church door: "Everyone concerned for the truth of the gospel is invited to be present at 9 A.M. outside the town walls, where the ungodly books supporting the Romanist claims will be burned. It may be that this is the time when the Antichrist is to appear."

The crowd gathered. One of the masters kindled the fire. To it were fed books of Roman Catholic theology, tracts against Luther, and, to the spectators' awe, the entire body of Roman Catholic canon law, the very legal foundations of the church of Rome. The flames mounted. As if suddenly reaching a decision, Luther stepped out from his colleagues. Deeply agitated, he solemnly cast the bull *Exsurge* into the fire, saying, "Because you have destroyed the truth of God, may the Lord consume you in these flames!" The professors then quietly returned home, but the students boisterously burned more books and paraded through the town until they had to be stopped the next day by the town authorities.

How to Handle a Heretic

Our scene now moves far away to the free city of Worms, on the west side of the Rhine near Heidelberg, where the youthful Emperor Charles V had gathered his first imperial diet. Here would take place the showdown on the case of Martin Luther.

Normally, handling a condemned heretic would be an insignificant matter. Law required that when the church declared its condemnation, the empire must immediately outlaw the heretic; anyone who turned him over to the state for burning, or even killed him, would earn the empire's gratitude.

But the times were far from normal. The thirty-seven-year-old "little monk" from Wittenberg understood most clearly of all what was at stake. "It is the cause of God, of universal Christendom, and of the whole German nation—not that of a single man, much less mine," he wrote to Frederick. The main issue was the gospel of Christ. Hence, "no one's danger, no one's safety can be considered here. We must rather take care not to expose the gospel to the mockery of the ungodly, and thus give our enemies a reason for boasting over us that we dare not confess what we have taught, and are afraid to shed our blood for it." The cause could only be commended to the Lord. But this did not mean, of course, that Luther discounted his friends' efforts; as he wrote to young Duke John Frederick, the elector's nephew: God in his providence often works his will through the deeds of princes.

The diet debated how to handle the Luther affair. On the floor and behind the scenes the diplomats conferred and plotted. In November the emperor had ordered Frederick to have Luther appear for a hearing; in December he retracted the order. The papal nuncio, Jerome Aleander, reminded the diet that laymen had no jurisdiction in such a case. Charles agreed. Constitutionally, however, no German was to be condemned unheard. Moreover, the people were in an ugly mood. "All Germany is in full revolt," said Aleander's dispatch to Rome. "Nine-tenths raise the war-cry 'Luther!' while the watchword of the other tenth who don't care about Luther is 'Death to the Roman Court!' "

In mid-February, hoping to forestall a hearing, Aleander orated for three hours on the enormity of Luther's heresy. The move backfired, in a sense, because in doing this he was virtually turning the assembly of laymen into a church council, making them judges of the case. The diet, meanwhile, feared that a popular revolt might be brewing. Emperor Charles therefore formally summoned the "honorable, dear, and pious Dr. Luther" to a hearing (what kind, he did not say), added his promise of a safe-conduct, and dispatched the imperial herald to Wittenberg. Now Aleander's task was to prevent the hearing from becoming a sounding board for Luther. He felt that the condemned heretic ought not to be allowed to speak, except to say whether he would recant or not.

The emperor's confessor had another thought. Perhaps Luther could be persuaded that an appearance at Worms would stir up war and please only the Devil; maybe a compromise settlement might prove attractive. Accordingly, the confessor tried to induce Luther's own friends, Hutten and his soldier-comrade Sir Francis von Sickingen, to persuade Luther to turn aside and remain in Sickingen's castle, where the matter could perhaps be settled informally. Hutten and Sickingen agreed to approach Luther on the subject. But again both foe and friend misread Luther. "I would go to Worms even if there were as many devils there as tiles on the roof." The journey proceeded almost like a triumphal procession. Luther preached in several towns, received warm hospitality, and accepted the greetings of large crowds.

Decision at Worms

Worms, April 16, 1521. The watchman in the cathedral spire announced by trumpet an important arrival. Preceded by the imperial herald, Dr. Luther and some friends in a horsedrawn Saxon cart rattled into the city. Two thousand people lined the streets. A cavalcade of horsemen escorted Luther to his lodgings. Alighting, he looked around ("with demoniac eyes," reported Aleander) and said, "God will be with me!"

April 17. At 4:00 P.M. Luther was led to the bishop's palace for the hearing. Still awed in the presence of the assembled princes, he heard the official spokesman address him on the gravity of the occasion. Then, pointing to a pile of twenty-five books on a table, the spokesman posed two sharp questions: "Do you acknowledge that these books are yours? And do you intend to defend and stand by them?" "Let the titles be read!" called out Frederick's lawyer.

Before the hushed audience, Luther's voice was low. He had read into the vague imperial summons a slender hope that his teachings might be heard and answered from Scripture. Instead he was simply being asked whether he recanted or not. "The books are all mine, and I have written others. As for the second question, however, that concerns faith and the salvation of souls, and the Word of God. To say too little or too much would be dangerous. Christ said, 'Whoever denies me before men, I also will deny before my Father.' Therefore I beg, with all respect, that your Imperial Majesty will give me time to think it over."

The diet deliberated. Finally the spokesman announced its decision. "Martin, you knew why you were summoned here. There is no reason why further time should be granted. Nevertheless, His Imperial Majesty graciously gives you one day to deliberate." Back in his lodgings Luther wrote, "With Christ's help, I shall not recant a single particle."

April 18. At 4:00 P.M. Luther was escorted to the diet, but he was not summoned into the meeting until 6 P.M. and candles were lit. The meeting was being held in a larger hall, but it was even more crowded. The spokesman repeated his questions. Luther now was a changed man. The miner's son stood without timidity before the descendant of emperors and kings, Emperor Charles, who had vowed, "This fellow will never make a heretic out of me!"

In a clear voice Luther spoke. "All my books are not of one kind." By this move he worked his way free of Aleander's intrigue.

"Some of them deal with faith and life so simply and evangelically that even my enemies must regard them as useful for Christians. . . . These I cannot recant without damning the truth which all confess. A second group assails the papacy, whose evil teaching and example have devastated the world. If I withdrew these books, I would open the door to more tyranny and ungodliness. A third class contains attacks on certain individuals who tore down my Christian teaching.

I admit that I have been more caustic than is becoming for a minister. But I am being judged not for my life, but for the teaching of Christ. I cannot renounce these works either, without promoting tyranny and ungodliness."

Briefed by the emperor's advisers, the spokesman retorted severely, "Luther, you have not answered to the point. Give a simple, unambiguous answer. Will you recant or not?"

"Your Majesty and Your Lordships ask for a plain answer. Unless I am convicted by scripture and plain reason—I do not accept the authority of popes or councils, since they have often contradicted one another—my conscience is captive to the Word of God. I cannot and will not recant anything, for to act against conscience is neither right nor safe. God help me! Amen."

"Here I stand, I cannot do otherwise!" These famous words do not stand in the eyewitness records, although they appear in the earliest printed accounts of the hearing. But whatever their origin, they are true to the spirit of the occasion.

The hall broke into an uproar. The imperial spokesman could not regain control of the situation. He and Luther exchanged sharp words. The emperor abruptly made a sign that the hearing was over. He swept out of the room and the meeting broke up. Surrounded by friends, Luther made his way to the door, as Spaniards hissed and shouted, "To the fire with him!" Outside, Luther happily raised both arms with outspread fingers—the gesture of a victorious German warrior. Greeted by comrades at his lodgings, he exclaimed with beaming face, "I am through! I am through!" In his own rooms Elector Frederick remarked, "Dr. Martin spoke well. But he is too bold for me!" That night the city rocked with excitement.

A Topsy-Turvy Business

The empire still had to dispose of the case. On the following day Charles called together a number of princes for their advice. They were unwilling to act in haste. "Very well," replied the emperor, "but I shall give you my own opinion." He then read to them a carefully prepared declaration. "A single friar contradicting all Christianity for a thousand years must be wrong. I am resolved to stake my lands, my friends, my body, my blood, my life, and my soul. Luther may return under his safe-conduct, but then I will proceed against him as a notorious heretic." That was a binding pledge for an emperor. Out in the streets, meanwhile, were hot-tempered placard-bearers. Among them appeared the sign of the "Peasant's Shoe," ominous threat of peasant revolt.

A few of the princes and archbishops, with Charles' reluctant consent, tried to salvage the Luther case by means of private arbitration. Here was a topsy-turvy business. First Luther had been sentenced, then the prosecutor had summed up, now came a hearing. To top everything, the diet had proceeded all this time without the official decree from Rome banning Luther. Aleander had received it, but for reasons of his own had sent it back for alterations.

For a week the princes and prelates negotiated with Luther. Their intentions were good. Could not Luther, on his part, give way just a little? The peace of the empire was at stake. Once Luther was on the verge of tears. The chief issue, however, remained unresolved, since the arbitrators did not undertake to correct Luther on the basis of the Word of God. Church reform efforts have never accomplished much when they have not started from the very heart of religion, the question of man's salvation.

Disappearance

On April 26, the imperial heralds escorted Luther through the city gates on his homeward journey. The princes, too, began to leave. The emperor waited quietly, gathering support. Finally, on May 26, he solemnly signed the Edict of Worms. Violently condemning Luther's teaching and his life as well, the edict decreed the ban of the empire upon "this devil in the garb of a monk" and upon all his followers. From now on, there was open season on Martin Luther.

The opposite side of the story came out in Luther's last words to the imperial arbitrators the evening before he left Worms. "I have sought nothing but a reformation of the church according to holy scripture. I would suffer death and infamy, give up life and reputation for His Imperial Majesty and the Empire. I make no reservation except the right to confess the Word of God." "The gospel of God," he wrote in a letter published soon afterwards, "this was the nub of the controversy."

Which side would prevail? Luther had always committed his cause to God. Now he and the rest of the world would see.

Early in May startling news exploded in Worms. On the way home Luther disappeared. Reports said he had been kidnapped.

Who was responsible? Some thought it was Aleander. "I only wish you were right!" he snapped. Aleander thought the outlaw was planning a revolt. A letter reached the city, saying that Luther's stabbed body had been found in a silver mine. Albrecht Dürer in Belgium wrote in his diary, "O God, if Luther is dead, who will explain the holy gospel for us?"

PART FOUR

Rebuilding

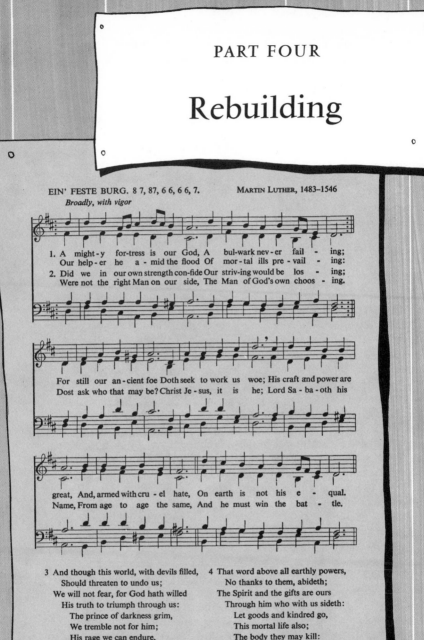

EIN' FESTE BURG. 8 7, 87, 6 6, 6 6, 7.   MARTIN LUTHER, 1483–1546

Broadly, with vigor

1. A might-y for-tress is our God, A bul-wark nev-er fail - ing;
Our help-er he a-mid the flood Of mor-tal ills pre-vail - ing:
2. Did we in our own strength con-fide Our striv-ing would be los - ing;
Were not the right Man on our side, The Man of God's own choos - ing.

For still our an-cient foe Doth seek to work us woe; His craft and power are
Dost ask who that may be? Christ Je-sus, it is he; Lord Sa-ba-oth his

great, And, armed with cru-el hate, On earth is not his e - qual.
Name, From age to age the same, And he must win the bat - tle.

3 And though this world, with devils filled,
   Should threaten to undo us;
We will not fear, for God hath willed
   His truth to triumph through us:
      The prince of darkness grim,
      We tremble not for him;
      His rage we can endure,
      For lo! his doom is sure,
One little word shall fell him.

4 That word above all earthly powers,
   No thanks to them, abideth;
The Spirit and the gifts are ours
   Through him who with us sideth:
      Let goods and kindred go,
      This mortal life also;
      The body they may kill:
      God's truth abideth still,
His kingdom is forever.

Martin Luther, 1483–1546
Tr. Frederick H. Hedge, 1805–90
Based on Psalm 46

20. Two Wildernesses

LUTHER was very much alive. Letters began to reach his friends, marked "From the land of the birds," "From the wilderness," or "From the Isle of Patmos." The latter was a reference to the exile of the author of Revelation. Where in the world was this hideaway? "Sorry," replied the man officially responsible for Luther's safety, "I honestly don't know."

It was true. Frederick, the old fox, had cleverly directed his aides to have Luther kidnapped and hidden somewhere unknown to him. After all, if Charles threatened to enforce the stern penalties of the Edict of Worms upon all Saxony because of Luther's disappearance, the elector needed to be ignorant of his whereabouts.

The aides planned cleverly, too. Seven days away from Worms, in the late afternoon, Luther's cart was rumbling through the lonely Thuringian forest. Suddenly a handful of armed horsemen galloped out of nowhere, roughly knocked the driver to the ground, and jerked Luther from the cart. Allowing the driver and Luther's other companion to drive on, the knights disappeared into the woods with their captive. Late in the evening Martin found himself settled in a room in the old Wartburg Castle on its perch overlooking Eisenach, where he had once gone to school.

Sir George

Luther had been in on the secret, but few others were, even at the castle. Needing to remain incognito, he let his hair and beard grow. He was dressed as a knight and addressed as Sir George. "I can't even recognize myself," he wrote to Spalatin, who had been let in on the secret.

He was safe for the moment. But what should he do now? Go back and court martyrdom, recant, stay safely in retirement, help prepare for public revolt or at least resistance to attack? None of these alternatives made much sense to Luther. "I've come through!" he had cried at Worms. But through for what? His one concern, his one goal, had been that the gospel of Christ should have free course among men. This remained his one great task.

Practically speaking, however, this goal required fresh thought. The situation he faced was an altogether new one. Until now, he had been clearing the ground; it is quite another thing to rebuild something better. A new, constructive kind of wisdom would be needed. Did he or anyone else have it? The medieval church had controlled the religious situation in Europe by tight regulations, backed up by imperial force. Without them, what power would produce order and stability?

Furthermore what would Luther's role be in the new era? "The movement is quite independent of Luther," Aleander had remarked even before Luther appeared at Worms. Of course, the movement was considerably bigger than Luther; it had always been so. Others beside him had yearned for reforms. Indeed, it was while Luther was out of the scene that the Reformation actually broke out—in the sense of drastic public changes. Since everybody had his own idea what these changes should be, who could guarantee that the gospel would remain the guiding star—or even that it would not be totally eclipsed?

The Mighty Pen

"I am rotting here, alone and half dead," Luther complained. "I sit here like a fool, hardened in leisure."

Wouldn't his "wilderness" solitude provide a welcome rest after all the tension of the last few weeks—and the last few years? Not for someone with a temperament like Luther's. He was kept generally in seclusion, although news of his whereabouts eventually leaked out. Messengers, meanwhile, kept him in close touch with happenings elsewhere and brought him books. For months he was plagued by illness, the beginning of severe ailments which were to become chronic. Illness in turn aggravated the "troubles of his soul." So did his concern for the church in the world he had fled. "I cannot shake off the worry that wolves may enter the sheepfold now that I am away." He feared that violence was coming. "Satan is threatening Germany with some deadly tragedy, and I fear the Lord will allow him to bring it about. Let us pray and watch."

"Hardening leisure," meanwhile, was hardly the description for Luther's ten months at the Wartburg. Though ill and away from his library, he wrote as busily as ever. Solid theological treatises flowed from his pen. Pamphlets exposed and attacked abuses in church practice. He blasted the rule that private confession of all sins is compulsory. He attacked the mighty monastic system head-on. It rested on the false assumption that a special religious "calling" is superior in worth to the calling of ordinary Christians. Moreover no such vows should be permanently binding. This treatise, *On Monastic*

Vows, said his colleague Justus Jonas, "is the work that emptied the cloisters." Luther attacked next the custom of endowment, "private Masses;" in the Castle Church, for instance, a staff of twenty-five priests was needed just to recite these Masses to gain God's favor for their beneficiaries. Luther insisted once more that the Lord's Supper is a communion, not a meritorious good work. Next, by threatening to publish an attack he had written against a new indulgence campaign of Archbishop Albert, he forced Albert to abandon it; the archbishop meekly promised that he would try to be a pious Christian prince.

Far more important in the long run were the writings designed to feed the hearts of common Christians. One beautiful example, dedicated to the teen-age Duke John Frederick, was Luther's explanation of the Magnificat, commending the humility of the Virgin Mary as a model of Christian faith and life. Luther had also been long at work writing sermons on the gospels and epistles of the church year. The people needed to hear God's Word explained regularly, and many priests had never been trained to preach. From Wartburg Castle Luther sent off to the printer his sermons for the Advent and Christmas seasons, and later he completed this *Church Postil,* so that sound sermons at least could be read to the people. He considered it one of his best books. It exercised an enormous influence on the devotional life of Germany for centuries.

Most significant of all, he translated the New Testament into German. "I wish," he wrote, "that this book alone, in all languages, would live in the hands, eyes, ears, and hearts of all people." "All other writings are meant to lead the way into the scriptures," he was to write later. "Don't let my books divert anyone from studying the scriptures themselves." Previous translations had existed, but Luther's translation far surpassed its predecessors in accuracy (since Luther for the first time translated out of the original Greek) and, best of all, in the majesty and rhythm and earthiness of its diction. With only a few books to aid him, Luther completed the entire first draft in eleven weeks. Published in September, 1522, the first edition of five thousand copies sold out in two months. By that time the careful scholar was already revising the translation and assembling a committee of colleagues to work on the Old Testament.

Violence

The violence Luther had feared began to break out—unhappily, right in Wittenberg. Professor Carlstadt and the fiery young monk Gabriel Zwilling had decided that church life needed to be changed from top to bottom. During the fall of 1521 they inaugurated a program of reforms in Wittenberg. The Mass is evil; don't attend it. Hear preaching instead, and take communion "in both kinds," bread and wine. Monasticism is evil; pray "in the Spirit" and don't let monastic rules get in your way. Better still, leave the monastery. In November, more than a dozen Augustinian monks—half of the company—followed Brother Gabriel's urging and left. The vow of celibacy is evil; priests and monks and nuns should get married. On Christmas Eve, Carlstadt conducted a communion service wearing no Mass vestments, and placed directly into the laymen's hands the bread and chalice from the altar.

At about the same time the "Zwickau Prophets," two devout weavers and a former Wittenberg student, who all claimed to have direct conversation with God, came to town and added fuel to the fire—repudiating infant baptism, disclaiming the importance of the Bible, and advocating the killing of the "ungodly." More and more, people were being urged to separate themselves completely from the Roman Catholic church and all of its trappings.

Luther, who had made a secret trip to Wittenberg earlier in December, was not too worried at first. Even if Carlstadt was unsteady, his other colleagues ought to be able to manage things. Most of all he counted on young Philipp Melanchthon to exercise leadership. Ever since his arrival at the university in 1518, the two had been warm friends. Their friendship remained firm throughout their lives, even though they did not see eye to eye on many theological matters. In this emotionally charged Wittenberg crisis, however, the slender little twenty-four-year-old scholar was too gentle and indecisive. To the elector's court he confessed, "These men ought to meet Luther. They appeal to him. . . . I don't know where these things will end, unless Luther intervenes. Where shall I turn?"

Things got far out of hand in January, 1522. Mobs, egged on by Carlstadt and Zwilling, tore down altars and images in the churches of Wittenberg and desecrated cemeteries. Now it was Frederick's turn to be confused, since his Wittenberg professors could not agree among themselves. Late in February he was still uncertain whether Luther ought to return, and he even asked Luther's advice. Wittenberg, where the gospel had been brought to light, had become a wilderness.

Back to Wittenberg

Luther waited no longer. Early in March he set out for Wittenberg, about a 175-mile journey, much of it through the lands of Duke

George the Bearded, who had just issued a stern order that all monks spreading the renegade Luther's teachings should be clapped into prison. On the way Martin wrote a letter to Frederick. "I would come, even if it rained Duke Georges for nine days. I am going to Wittenberg under a far higher protection than the Elector's. I have no intention of asking Your Electoral Grace for protection. Indeed, I think I shall protect Your Electoral Grace more than you can protect me. The sword ought not and cannot help a matter of this kind. God alone must do it."

On Thursday, March 6, Luther arrived in Wittenberg. The town buzzed with excitement. "Dr. Luther is going to preach on Sunday." Some expected a riot to develop. But they were mistaken.

Calmly and pointedly Luther spoke from his pulpit about the essentials of the Christian life: recognition of sin, faith, love, patience and forbearance with one another. "Without love faith is nothing. Here, dear friends, have you not grievously failed? I see no signs of love among you." To reform the Mass was right, but the Wittenbergers had done it in a disorderly way and offended many. What is "free" dare not be made into a new "must," he pointed out. The sermon was quickly over. "Tomorrow we shall deal with images."

The people listened soberly and came back the next day. "I will preach, teach, write, but I will constrain no man by force, for faith must come freely without compulsion. Take myself as an example. I opposed indulgences and all the papists, but never with force. I simply taught, preached, and wrote God's Word; otherwise I did nothing. The Word did it all. Had I desired to stir up trouble, I could have brought great bloodshed upon Germany; even the emperor would not have been safe. But what would that have been? Mere fool's play. So I did nothing; I let the Word do its work." For eight successive days Luther preached brief sermons about religious affairs in Wittenberg. "No new practices should be introduced until the gospel has been thoroughly preached and understood," he summarized.

The effect of his sermons was amazing. A professor of law reported to Frederick, "There is great happiness here, among both the learned and the unlearned, over Dr. Martin's return and over the sermons with which, by God's help, he is daily pointing us poor deluded men back again to the way of truth, showing us beyond question the pitiful errors into which we have been led by the preachers who forced their way among us. Even Gabriel [Zwilling] has confessed that he erred and went too far." The town returned to quiet and order. Luther recommended a pastorate for the hothead

Zwilling, who eventually turned in a record of useful service. Unreconstructed, Carlstadt and the "Zwickau Prophets" departed. Disorder, meanwhile was threatening not only in Wittenberg but also in Thuringia. On a secret journey there in December, Luther had been alarmed to find the peasants on the verge of open revolt. He rushed a tract through the press in January to warn all Christians "against riot and rebellion." His message was similar to the one given to Wittenberg. "Riot is an unprofitable way to proceed. It never results in the desired reform. Those who understand my teaching correctly will not cause a riot." In any case, no revolt took place for the time being. But time was running out.

Discord

Luther was right that trouble was coming. But he had expected the papacy to start it and God to handle it. "Wait," he told both commoners and rulers in the tract against riot, "preach the gospel, tell men that a Christian life consists of faith and love. Do this for two years longer and you will see what will become of pope, bishops, priests, monks, masses, rules, and the whole rotten mess of the papal government—they will all vanish like smoke!" But Luther was off target on two counts. First, he underestimated the papacy's true strength; and second, this violence started within his own camp. Many deep motivations besides Christian liberty were at work among his people.

These disturbances proved one thing, however. The Edict of Worms was unenforceable. The riots had taken place precisely during Luther's absence. The authorities realized, therefore, that killing Luther would only bring greater disorders. For better or worse, even the hostile Duke George at this moment could only hope and trust that Luther would guide these forces into constructive channels.

21. Steps on the Middle Way

RESTORING order could not mean restoring all the old church practices. Things had gone too far for that. Not only in Saxony, but in faraway places, men were urging changes. In more and more places, preaching services and communion instead of the Mass became the center of worship, the cup was given to the laity, worship was conducted in German instead of Latin.

Although many of the changes were good, they were not being made on any systematic basis. There seemed little to prevent the whole church life from plunging into chaos. How could some order and stability be brought into the "evangelical" movement ("evangelical" means following the gospel) without trying to force uniformity, and without stifling the very gospel on which it was based? There had to be a middle course between moving too fast and too slowly, between confusing the "may" with the "must." The main problem for the leaders of the people of Christ was, after all, to get them to hear God's true Word, and truly to worship and obey the God who spoke it.

Clearly seeing the need, Luther set about to fulfill it, not only by his own labors, but by enlisting his colleagues. The Wittenbergers and their friends elsewhere went to work industriously to provide the equipment for an evangelical church life. We have already mentioned devotional books, commentaries on the Bible, books of sermons, and the Bible translation itself. Now they must produce orders of worship in harmony with the pure gospel.

Forms of Worship

In 1523 Luther put his own hand to the task. For a neighboring town which had consulted him on how to order its congregational worship, he wrote a memorandum emphasizing that daily training in the Word of God and prayer for the fruits of the Word should be the key principles. Next he produced a German order for Baptism, his first effort to put worship into the language of the common people. After that he wrote a Latin Communion liturgy, moderately revising the Roman Catholic Mass in order to present the sacrament as God's gracious gift to us, and to accompany it with the preaching of the Word.

This was only a beginning. In subsequent years both Luther and others continued polishing the forms of worship, for he was convinced that public worship is "the greatest and most loving service we can perform for God," and at the same time the greatest "power" the church has. A quick glance at Luther's thoughts on common worship will show how rich and deep was his concern.

The heart of all worship is the Word of God. In worship the Word is offered and received, and to it we respond. Preaching God's commands and his promises therefore assumes a position of tremendous importance. For Luther, however, this does not mean the one-sided emphasis on sermons which has frequently overtaken Protestantism, once tersely described as: "And the Word became *words.*" Luther regarded preaching and the Sacraments of Baptism and the Lord's Supper as two forms of the same Word, one spoken and one enacted, and he tried to keep them in lively balance. At the main Sunday morning service he wanted a sermon on the gospel for the day, and then Communion for all who felt the need for it. It must also be remembered that Luther envisioned other Sunday services and weekday services, most of which would be devoted simply to common prayer and preaching, the latter based on the epistles or going through a book of the Bible or explaining parts of the catechism.

Although a good liturgy is a valuable aid to worship, it belongs to the realm of "may," not of "must." It dare not, Luther emphasized, be imposed as something necessary, for it is devised by men, not commanded by God. Church authorities in a given area, he said, must decide what forms of worship will best "edify," that is, "build up" the church (to use Paul's word). Melanchthon, in his *Apology of the Augsburg Confession,* expressed the Lutheran sense of balance beautifully: "The true unity of the church is not harmed by variety in rites established by men, but we are pleased when common rites are observed for the sake of tranquility."

Luther tried to retain the old familiar forms, changing only what he found contrary to the Word or unedifying. In this he contrasted sharply with many other reformers who, with the purpose of making worship truly "spiritual," abolished all the old forms they could, retaining only what the Word explicitly commanded. If an old form still edified, thought Luther, why abolish it?

Luther's chief concern was for the church, the community of Christians gathered in Christ's name. Public worship is not merely private prayers performed together. It is the body of Christ as a living unit coming before God in adoration and petition and receiving power from God. All Christians together are "the priesthood," offering prayer and praise to God and intercession for others, even if one Christian may be assigned the office of leader in worship and preaching. It is therefore all the more important for the entire congregation to understand the service and to take as active a part in it as possible.

This same conviction also led Luther to urge musicians and poets to provide hymns for the common people. So successful was this that the Lutheran church became known as "the singing church." Indeed, its enemies observed that the Reformation "sang its way into the hearts of the people." As early as 1524 the first evangelical hymnals appeared, one containing twenty-four hymns by Luther himself. Some were translations of old hymns; some, like "Out of the Depths," were modeled on the psalms; some were his own in-

112

spiration, including probably his first hymn, a song of consolation upon the burning of the first two Lutheran martyrs at Brussels in 1523. Though not an expert musician, he was skillful enough to write the powerful melody of "A Mighty Fortress" and several others.

Luther also saw the need of religious instruction for the common people. He and others had written popular tracts before. Now, in 1525, he asked two colleagues to work on "catechisms" to teach the elements of the Christian faith to children and house servants. But in this area immediate results were meager until Luther undertook the task himself in 1529.

Toward Better Education

Still more urgent, meanwhile, was the whole problem of common education in Protestant lands. Luther had already called the attention of the nobility to the need of good schools for both boys and girls. Poor schools in the past had produced mainly ignorant priests "fit neither to cackle nor to lay eggs." This was why Germany had remained so backward. In many places what schools there were had collapsed because the income that supported them was cut off by the Reformation. Carlstadt, after leaving Wittenberg, contributed to the chaos by a wild "spiritual" teaching which disparaged education itself: God comes to Christians directly, therefore book-learning is arrogantly unspiritual. He, the former university dean of theology, went about asking illiterate peasants the meaning of biblical passages, since they, too, may have the Spirit.

A desperate crisis had developed. Luther addressed himself to it. In 1524 he issued a spirited summons to city councilmen all over Germany to establish Christian schools, "that the world may be made better." "Today we are living in a new era," he cried. "The world must have good and skilled men and women." It was indispensable for the church to have able, educated ministers. Society needed men trained in law, medicine, teaching, and other professions. Indeed, wrote Luther in 1530, it is more urgent to send able boys into law than into preaching. The minister has his basic message given him in the Word, but in governing for the welfare of all the people, a civil servant must "shoot in the dark," using his reason resourcefully.

In any case all honorable callings are God's own orders. Parents are set by God over families, pastors are "spiritual fathers," princes and civil servants are fathers of the state, honest workmen are the hands by which God provides life for the world. Good schools are God's means to educate such men and women for service to society.

So energetically did Lutheran pastors and governments tackle this discouraging task of popular education that in time Germany was set upon the path to its subsequent cultural greatness. Melanchthon and Bugenhagen were the great architects who designed the school systems which made Lutheranism a church with a high regard for education. Other Protestants followed and furthered the educational ideal. Not until Ignatius Loyola's Society of Jesus (commonly called the Jesuits) was established in 1541 did Roman Catholics begin to rival Protestants in popular education.

Luther's hopes were modest in details. For ordinary youngsters, for instance, he hoped for an hour or two daily in school, then work at home or in an apprenticeship. Luther's larger ideals, however, gave a powerful thrust to educational efforts. Trades and professions were accorded high dignity. Service to common society was recognized as a blessing to God greater than the prayers of monks and nuns. Paternalistic though Luther was in his social outlook, he had a vision of the rise of the common people. "Have your son study, and you are giving our Lord God a fine bit of wood out of which he can carve you a nobleman. Your son and my son—the sons of common folk—will inevitably rule the world, both in the spiritual and civil realms" (1530).

Social and Political Advisor

Luther even turned his hand to social and political advice. Though he usually did so only when he was consulted by towns or princes, still he spoke out whenever he saw abuses crying for correction. One great need was for some sort of social welfare program. Previously the monasteries had been the chief agents of charity to the poor, and even begging had been an accepted profession. Now the monasteries themselves were closing down, the monks and nuns were swelling the ranks of the jobless, and the profession of beggar had been abolished. All right, wrote Luther, if towns and princes seize the property and income of monasteries, let them use these to support a "common chest" and other programs of welfare.

In the economic realm Luther also wrote to urge what we today would call "fair trade" and "fair price."

Most important, Luther wrote on the question of government and citizenship. German society, suddenly loosed from old authorities and old patterns of life, was verging on chaos. Luther's treatise of 1523, *Civil Authority: How It Should Be Obeyed,* made a tremendous contribution to the reshaping and stabilizing of the country. In medieval Europe there had been an overlapping of church and state.

Bishops of the church, for example, were also feudal princes ruling vast lands. The church claimed complete authority over the spiritual realm—and applied the word "spiritual" to everything it controlled. At the same time, it claimed that civil government was subject to its spiritual guidance.

The Two Realms

Luther, on the other hand, taught that there are two sharply distinct realms, the spiritual and the civil. Both of them are established by God, and he ultimately rules both. But his two realms have different purposes and operate in different ways. A tract which he wrote in 1526 expresses the distinction with brilliant brevity. "The one kind of government is spiritual; it has no sword, but it has the Word, by means of which men are to become good and righteous, so that with this righteousness they may attain everlasting life. The other is worldly government through the sword, in order that if people are unwilling to become good and righteous unto eternal life through the Word, they may nevertheless be forced by this civil government to be good and just before the world. This kind of justice God administers through the sword, in order that peace may be kept among men, and he rewards it with earthly blessings. Thus God himself is the founder, lord, master, protector and rewarder of both kinds of righteousness. Each is an altogether divine thing."

It is disastrous to confuse these realms. If it is ruinous to the church to run it in a worldly, legalistic way, it would be equally disastrous to try to run the state by the gospel's simple precepts of love. It would be "like a shepherd who put together in one fold wolves, lions, eagles, and sheep, and let them mingle freely with one another, saying, 'Help yourselves, and be good and peaceful toward one another. The fold is open, there is plenty of food. Have no fear of dogs and clubs.' The sheep would doubtless keep the peace, but they would not live long. Neither would one beast survive another. For this reason one must carefully distinguish between these two governments. Both must be permitted to remain; the one to produce righteousness, the other to bring about external peace and prevent evil deeds. Neither one is sufficient in the world without the other."

Under God, then, each realm has its own standard: The church properly lives by love, the gentle law of Christ; the state administers justice or equity (fairness) by means of reason or firm common sense. This is not to exclude mercy from the law, for mercy is necessary to fairness. The main point, however, is that if men are to live together in this world, justice must be maintained whether some people wish so or not, and justice requires a government which can curb the unruly and promote the peace and welfare of society.

If the state must "wield the sword"—that is, have force at its disposal—must true Christians obey it? And may Christians take government posts as prince, judge, lawmaker, or soldier? Certainly. Civil government is instituted by God; obedience to it, as a service to God's children, is a service to God. Christians above all others should offer themselves for government service, knowing its importance in God's ordering of the world.

Luther wrote his treatise to show that civil government is responsible directly to God and is not under the church's supervision. He aimed to hearten and strengthen civil authorities to do their duty for the good of society. Moreover he aimed to teach the people the essentials of law-abiding citizenship. Many critics have accused Luther, because of this treatise, of leading the German people into blind obedience to the state. Curiously, the criticism hurled at him in his day was the opposite. When Luther wrote that princes are often fools, that the government is limited to the things of the body and cannot touch the soul, and that a Christian whose ruler clearly commands him to disobey God must rather disobey his ruler, Duke George read the tract as an ungodly summons to civil revolt.

22. Hopes and Harsh Realities

OUT of the confusion and groping and jockeying of persons and parties in the 1520's, a clear dual pattern eventually began to emerge. On the one hand, the Reformation was spreading. On the other hand, forces which in 1521 had supported Luther were moving away.

The Spreading Reformation

Even to his dying day in 1525, cautious old Elector Frederick never openly declared Electoral Saxony evangelical, but his brother John on succeeding him promptly did so. By that time several other powers had come out publicly on the evangelical side. Many free cities elected to support the Reformation. Often led by the cultural patricians, almost always pressed by the artisans and small merchants, cities like Nuremberg, Augsburg, and Strassburg in the south, Lübeck and Hamburg in the north, were beginning to embrace the evangelical faith.

The Reformation also made headway in the larger states. In northern Germany the Grand Master of the Teutonic Knights, a semi-monastic military order, converted his lands into a secular duchy of Prussia in 1525 and espoused Lutheranism. Hesse in central Germany was on the verge of change. Denmark and Sweden, though hostile to each other, were both tending toward the Lutheran faith. Some bishops even considered moves like that of the Teutonic Order.

Lost Enthusiasm

Harsh realities soon tempered the hopes of the reformers. Nine-tenths of Germany is on Luther's side, Aleander had declared in 1521. But this alliance proved to be an unstable one. First Sickingen and the petty knights engaged in a foolish armed uprising against the Archbishop of Trier which collapsed within one year. In 1523 Sickingen was killed and Hutten was forced to flee to Switzerland, where he died. Luther viewed Sickingen's death as a judgment of God. He had no sympathy with such rebellions, especially when they used the gospel as a tool for their own ends.

Many of the religious reformers were dissatisfied with Luther's understanding of the gospel. Carlstadt thought it was not spiritual enough. Others thought that with its emphasis on faith, it was not morally earnest enough. To the young firebrand Thomas Müntzer, the "Dr. Easychair" and "Dr. Pussyfoot" of Wittenberg was not aggressive enough for God's cause. Expelled from a pastorate in Zwickau, Müntzer developed into a religious revolutionary. He claimed direct visions from God and scorned Luther's bondage to the written Word. Guided by his "inner Word," he had the audacity to preach before the princes of Saxony, "the sword is given to you to wipe out the ungodly. If you refuse, it will be taken from you. The godless have no right to live." The princes took a dim view of this message, but Müntzer's fiery eloquence won a considerable following among the people.

A sizeable group of the humanists also withdrew their support of Luther. Men of culture had supported Luther enthusiastically in his early attack against abuses and in his struggle for freedom of thought and speech. Now, however, many were disturbed by the rising strife and the evidence of moral ineffectiveness that they saw. The followers of Erasmus had a better and simpler program to offer. Education in the teachings of Christ will bring out the better nature in man. Peace, not tumult, is the spirit of Christ. Not surprisingly, many of the humanists felt that the old order offered a firmer foundation for peace than the new one.

Erasmus, who had remained fairly neutral during the religious conflict, finally attacked Luther in 1524 with a treatise on man's free will. Within a year Luther retorted with his famous, often misunderstood, treatise on the *Bondage of the Will*. Luther clearly recognized that men always have the power of choice. But he insisted that man is not free genuinely to love God and love his neighbor until Christ sets him free from his self-will. A dog on a leash has plenty of choices, but he is still bound to the leash. For Luther, true faith and love are not the result of an appeal to our better nature. They are a wondrous miracle of God's gracious gift in Christ. This was the same message that Luther had been forging from the time of his Romans lectures of 1515.

The Peasants' War

Just then fell the most violent and disastrous blow of all upon the young Reformation—the Peasants' War of 1524–25. So complex was this revolt that it almost defies understanding to this day. How much more dimly and distortedly, then, did the rulers, Luther, and the peasants themselves understand the forces that unleashed it. In one sense it was simply the climax of almost two centuries of peasant uprisings in France, the Low Countries, England, and Germany. In part the peasants' demands were conservative: They were protesting against changes in laws, changes in labor conditions, monetary inflation, and other invasions of the rights their grandparents had once known. At one time, for example, forests and streams had been considered common property; now it was said that they belonged to the nobles personally, and fishing, hunting, and gathering firewood were restricted. By and large, it was not the most downtrodden peasants who began the revolt, but ones who had enjoyed some advantages which now were being taken away from them.

A striking feature of this particular peasant revolt was the strong religious note pervading it. From medieval sects the peasant leaders drew visions of the equality of all men before God, and a "heavenly kingdom" of the poor man. To these visions they attached Luther's idea of the priesthood of all believers in Christ. Luther's theme of Christian liberty they transposed into liberation from feudal exploitation. Willy-nilly, Luther found himself a symbol of the peasants' aspirations. Convinced of God's favor, "Poor Conrad" the peasant sharpened his knife in secret and made ready his scythe or his flail.

In the summer of 1524 the peasants' patience snapped. Beginning in the southwestern corner of Germany, the revolt smoldered for a few months, then burst out and spread like a prairie fire. With no clear program and no unity, the peasants left themselves open to the leadership of demagogues and plunderers. By the spring of 1525 most of upper Germany and Austria were aflame and violence was increasing. Castles, monasteries, and convents were pillaged, countrysides were terrorized. In Franconia (the region around Nuremberg) powerful Catholic bishoprics were the targets. In Thuringia, near Luther's birthplace, Thomas Müntzer whipped up the peasants with his eloquence, "On, on, on! Pay no attention to the cries of the godless. On, while the fire is hot. Let not the blood grow cold on your sword!"

Peasants of Swabia, in the southwest, did try to give positive direction and unity to the movement by publishing a proclamation, *The Twelve Articles,* in March, 1525. Generally sane and moderate, especially to modern ears, the *Articles* claimed that their demands were based on "the divine law," on "brotherly love and the Holy Scriptures." The peasants may have gotten the idea of lifting up the gospel as the banner of social revolt from so-called "Lutheran" preachers here and there, but not from Luther. Nevertheless the peasants appealed to Luther and other reformers by name, to act as judges of their demands. Now he had to speak.

Luther's Reaction

Luther spoke and acted with characteristic promptness and vigor. In April he answered *The Twelve Articles* with an *Admonition to Peace.* Some of the peasants' demands he called fair and just. He scorched the princes and bishops: "We have no one on earth to thank for this mischievous rebellion but you. In your states you do nothing but skin and rob your subjects." God's wrath was on its way. In equally sharp terms, however, he warned the peasants that "All who take the sword shall perish by the sword."

But he was too late. By the time his tract came out, the moderate peasants had lost all control. A massacre had been reported, a count had been murdered, Müntzer's mobs were terrorizing Thuringia. At the risk of his life Luther launched a preaching tour into the riot-torn area. But 1525 was not 1522. At one place Müntzer's followers rang the town bells to drown out the voice of the Wittenberg "Brother Fatted Pig." Elector Frederick, on his death bed, worried whether princes should do anything at all but meekly bear the rod of God's wrath.

Returning home on May 6, Luther dashed off the most bitter and violent pamphlet of his career, *Against the Thieving, Murdering Hordes of Peasants.* If the peasants refuse to come to terms, he wrote,

119

"let everyone who can, strike, slay, and stab, secretly or openly. Nothing can be more devilish than a rebel. It is just as when you must kill a mad dog. This is a time of the sword, not the day of grace." On three counts he indicted the rebels: Sedition is wrong; robbery and murder are wrong; worst of all, taking up the sword in the name of Christ's gospel is sheer blasphemy against God, a fatal confusion between the rights of human justice and the gentle way of Christ.

This tract, with all its fearful passion and its lack of pastoral sympathy, also came out too late. On May 15 the Thuringian peasants were crushed at the Battle of Frankenhausen, and Müntzer was executed. Other rebel bands collapsed within a short time. When Luther's harsh pamphlet appeared, the princes and bishops were already mopping up the countryside and executing rebels mercilessly. Luther's tract looked like beating a man already down. His enemies accused him of turning on a bloodbath. Urged to answer them, he wrote a further tract, but in it he refused to apologize. That would only confuse the matter more. He simply pointed out that he had urged mercy to peasants who came to terms, but not to those who stubbornly continued to rebel. Once again he reminded men that God strictly requires obedience to the government.

Collapse of the Revolt

The Peasants' War speedily collapsed. The results were fateful for the Reformation and for Germany. The peasants, bitterly disillusioned with Luther, in large measure forsook him. Had they ever really understood his message? Politically, the peasants lost all hope of improving their condition in Germany. As one historian says, "For three centuries they became hornless oxen." The princes tightened their control upon the land in both civil and religious affairs. The Roman Catholics tried to saddle Luther with responsibility for the entire revolt in order to prove that the Reformation was totally subversive. Evangelicals retorted that the rebellion had been far worse in lands ruled by bishops and abbots.

Luther on his part refused to falter. No longer was he the popular hero he had once been. He in turn lost his earlier trust in *Herr Omnes*, the common man, and his hope for a sweeping "improvement of Christian society." But he had remained basically true to himself. Now as before he consistently refused to let his religious reformation be transformed into a social or political program or used as a means to other ends. His firm but unhappily harsh stand during the Peasants' War left its marks on the Reformation, but also saved it as a religious movement. Not all was lost. Amid the harsh realities, hope remained. Indeed, it is a mistake to suppose that the Lutheran Reformation ceased to be a popular movement. Especially in the towns and cities, and even in some rural areas, the people's support persisted and grew.

23. Stabilizers

THE curtain had come up on a new scene in the Germany of the early 1520's. Some regions had decided to turn evangelical. They needed to rebuild their church life from the ground up. They needed protection from chaos in their midst and enemies around them.

With a mixture of Christian faithfulness and greedy self-interest, the evangelical governments groped their way toward stability. The Catholic powers who wanted to enforce the Edict of Worms were deterred by fears of revolt. The emperor could not bring pressure; he was engaged in a war—the first of several—with the "Most Christian" king of France. His Holiness, the pope, could not do much. After Leo's death late in 1521, a Dutchman, Adrian VI, had become the last non-Italian to wear Peter's triple crown. Adrian tried to reform the papal court, but died in less than a year, sorrowfully aware that Rome was not ready to be reformed. His successor, Clement VII, Leo's nephew, was merely an Italian prince who pursued pleasure and tried to undermine the Hapsburg emperor.

Divided Camps

The German princes, each jealous of his own privileges, were stalemated on the religious question. The evangelical powers called for a free church council to settle the issue, but the papacy had no intention of calling a council in Germany. German Catholic princes formed two alliances, one in the south and one in the north. The evangelical powers had little choice but to form a league of their own in 1525, led by Elector John of Saxony, brother and successor of Frederick, and twenty-one-year-old Landgrave Philip of Hesse. The formation of the league was made all the more urgent because their enemy Charles had greatly strengthened his position by capturing King Francis of France and dictating the peace.

Fortunately Charles had to turn his troops against Pope Clement VII, Francis' ally, and this kept the emperor busy until the sack of Rome in 1527, and for two years afterward. In the meantime the evangelical powers pushed through a significant resolution at the Diet of Speyer in 1526. The resolution stated that until a general council should meet in Germany to settle the religious question, each state should handle the issue "as it hoped to answer for its conduct to God and to the emperor." The Evangelicals interpreted this resolution as granting them freedom to reform their territories. Except for three important states, almost all of northern Germany turned Lutheran within three years.

For good and ill, princes and city councils were exerting their influence as stabilizers upon Lutheran Reformation. A day of reckoning was coming, however. Germany was divided into two hostile camps. At a time when no one could imagine a land permitting more than one form of religion, there did not seem to be any possibility of a settlement in Germany without a clash of arms.

Luther's Marriage

While the larger political situation was thus developing, Luther and his friends were also doing what they could to promote peace and stability. Indeed, it was actually as a gesture of hope and stability that on June 13, 1525, Luther married a former nun, Katherine von Bora. Some of his friends were embarrassed that he should suddenly marry during the tension and torment of the Peasants' War, but Luther saw the matter differently. Half a year earlier, he had told a friend that he did not expect to take a wife, "because I daily await the death decreed to the heretic." Now, amid greater danger, he changed his mind and married in order, he said, to please his father, to practice what he had preached, and to spite the Devil. Logical reasons, if not romantic ones.

Luther's marriage, in its own way, provided a stabilizing influence in the evangelical movement. The Roman Catholic church taught that priests, monks, and nuns had to remain unmarried, chiefly because celibacy was more holy than marriage. Luther's treatise *On Monastic Vows* sharply attacked this argument. It also denied that the church had the right to forbid its servants to marry; a voluntary choice to remain unmarried is one thing, but no one has a right to require it as a divine regulation. The true divine order is that most men and women need each other. God established and blessed marriage; Scripture does not show him commanding celibacy for the church's servants. For Roman Catholics the monastery was the model for saintly living; for Protestants, now, a far more God-pleasing model was the Christian family and home. Many of Luther's colleagues agreed with this advice and took wives. Luther himself followed tardily. Together Luther and his friends established an important new influence in society, the Protestant parsonage family. Still more important, Luther gave new depth to the Christian understanding of the commandment, "Honor your father and your mother."

The circumstances of Luther's marriage sound amusing today. In April, 1523, when cloisters were being emptied under the influence of Luther's teaching, nine nuns who had escaped from their nunnery came to Wittenberg. "A wretched crowd," wrote Luther. They were destitute. He and his colleagues tried to find places and support for them, and then virtually set up a marriage bureau to provide them husbands. At last only one was left, Katherine von Bora. Luther suggested that she marry a certain Pastor Glatz, who was available and, apparently, interested. Distressed, Katie went to Luther's friend Dr. Amsdorf and asked him to help her talk Luther out of the match. "I can't stand Dr. Glatz," Katie said, "but I would take either you or Dr. Luther." Shortly after this, when Luther visited his parents during his preaching tour in April, old Hans again urged him to marry. Martin finally took the idea seriously.

And so they were married, the forty-one-year-old reformer and the wellborn twenty-six-year-old ex-nun. It was no love match, but great affection and tenderness soon developed in their home and grew through the years. "I am not infatuated," said Luther, "but she is very dear to me." Later he remarked banteringly, "I would not exchange Katie for France or Venice. God has given her to me. Besides, other women have worse faults."

Family Life

In willpower Katie was a good match for the obstreperous doctor. He realized it, showing his respect when he referred to her as "Lord Katie," and even as "Kette," which means "chain" in German. As a bachelor Luther had neglected himself in many ways, not least in his health habits. Katie took care of him and polished off a few of his rough edges. She also proved a conscientious mother and a careful housekeeper. It was not easy for them to make ends meet, even after his salary was doubled and the rambling Augustinian monastery building was formally given to them by the elector to be their home. At one time or another there were over a dozen needy relatives for Katie to care for besides her own children. The Luthers took student boarders to supplement their income. It was to these students that we owe the priceless collection of almost 6600 anec-

dotes, the *Table Talk,* which take us so intimately into Luther's experiences and thoughts. Meanwhile the doctor also had enormous responsibilities in entertaining visitors, the great and humble. All this meant extra work for Katie. Once Prince George of Anhalt was considering a visit to Wittenberg. He received a letter which modified his plans: "Luther's home is occupied by a motley crowd of boys, students, girls, widows, old women, and youngsters, so there is much disturbance in the place. His house would offer you pleasant accommodations for a few days, but as the situation now stands, I would not advise that your Grace stop there."

The Luthers managed, however. Martin kept a vegetable garden; Katie kept an orchard, livestock, and a fish pond; and later managed a couple of small farms. Gifts also helped out, some of them handsome, like the wedding present of twenty gulden from Archbishop Albert. But Katie still had her troubles with her openhearted—and openhanded—husband. Once he proposed to give away a vase as a wedding gift; Katie hid it.

The Luthers had six children who were born between 1526 and 1534. One died in infancy; another, lovely little Magdalena, died at the age of thirteen. Their son Paul grew up to become a physician. We shall see a little more of Luther's family later.

New Reformers

By 1525 Carlstadt was discredited and Müntzer was dead, but many new reformers had stepped forth, spreading a variety of teachings. Most of them staunchly appealed to the Bible, though a man like Müntzer, as we saw, claimed a still higher authority. On many points, apparently, the Bible did not teach as unambiguously as Luther had thought. Or were all these teachers simply blind or misguided? In any case no one could force them to accept Luther's interpretations. Some of the new teachers, indeed, sharply criticized Luther for not going far enough to purify the church. They called him a Moses who led the children of Israel out of bondage but could not bring them into the Promised Land.

Zwingli's Swiss reformation and the Anabaptist movement were by far the most important new religious forces that appeared at this time. Both were attaining fairly stable form, and their influence was spreading.

Zwingli

Ulrich Zwingli, two months younger than Luther, had spearheaded an independent reformation in the Swiss city-state of Zurich. In a series of public debates, 1523–24, his eloquent evangelical message had won the government's verdict over his Roman Catholic opponents: Christ alone is our salvation through faith, and Scripture alone is our final authority in the faith. At the same time, with his humanist training, Zwingli was convinced that Christianity is a religion of clear good sense; as he later remarked to Luther at the Marburg Colloquy: "God does not ask us to believe many incomprehensible things."

Zwingli therefore became irritated over Luther's constant emphasis on the mysterious hidden ways of God which pass all human understanding. His irritation came into focus on Luther's view of the Lord's Supper. "This is my body; this is my blood," Christ had said in instituting the Holy Supper. Luther accepted this word literally, even if human reason cannot comprehend it. From 1524 on, Zwingli attacked Luther as a false reformer, still caught in the old nets of Catholicism. To Zwingli's way of thinking, Christ's body cannot possibly be present in the sacrament, because it has ascended into heaven; and even if it could be present, it would do us no good, because Christ said in John 6:63, "It is the spirit that gives life, the flesh is of no avail." Christ must have meant merely, "This bread signifies or symbolizes my body."

Zwingli and his friends kept up the attack in pamphlet after pamphlet. Luther had written strongly against Carlstadt's somewhat similar view in 1525. He was reluctant to reply to Zwingli. Eventually, however, he had to do it. He declared that just because Christ's body is not in the sacrament in a form which we can see and measure, that does not prove it is not present. Further, it is blasphemy to say that Christ's flesh does us no good. Christ came into human flesh to save us. The verse in John refers to what we would call "fleshliness" or worldliness.

Luther's careful argument did not alter the Swiss reformer's mind. The two were clearly divided. For Zwingli it was a question of a clear-cut, sensible, spiritual faith; it is Christ's spirit, not his flesh, that saves us. For Luther it was a question of humbly accepting God's gift of his Son in the way God gave him; Christ—the only Christ we know, spirit and body united—saves us, and it is this Christ himself whom we receive in the Supper.

Back and forth the controversy raged, reaching a peak in the lengthy and bitter treatises of 1528. What would it do to Protestant unity? The answer is painful. A wall would be erected between the Lutherans and the Reformed churches, which include the Presbyterian and Congregational traditions.

"Rebaptizers"

Other reformers, meanwhile, had as much trouble with Zwingli as he had with Luther. The religious scene seemed like a free-for-all, with as many teachings as teachers. Out of the confusion emerged an enduring group called by their enemies Anabaptists, which means "rebaptizers." These were the ancestors of the modern Mennonites and, indirectly, of the Baptists. Rising in Zurich in 1523, they criticized Zwingli for not carrying his reforms far enough. They were eager to restore the pattern of the primitive church—a close-knit, disciplined, morally earnest little flock. Their "gathered church" would be united, not by a creed, but by a code, the Sermon on the Mount obeyed literally, even if it meant suffering for their faith. They could find no warrant in Scripture for baptizing infants; Baptism, they held, is the sign of the believer's pledge to obey Christ. The Zurich "Brethren" therefore solemnly administered this rite to one another.

Suffering soon came. A similar group a thousand years earlier had been wiped out by the Christian Roman Empire. The law was still in force: Whoever rebaptizes is guilty of blasphemy against God and sedition against the state. From 1526 on, Zwingli, other Protestants, and Roman Catholics invoked the death penalty upon Anabaptists—usually by drowning, since they were so fond of water. The Anabaptists spread anyway, becoming numerous in Austria and southern Germany, where they were suspected of having been mixed up with the revolutionary peasants.

Luther, too, was sure that the Anabaptists were not only wrong, but dangerous "fanatics." What was he to think, for instance, when some men mocked Lutheran baptism as "a dog's bath," and defied the judges before whom they were tried? Two pastors asked Luther to express his opinion of Anabaptism. He replied in 1528 that infant baptism was the best possible sign that God takes the initiative to save us. We do not climb up into God's favor; he adopts the child into his holy family and nurtures him in a growing faith. Anabaptists were turning God's wondrous gift into a human performance. Moreover, if adult baptism were necessary to keep the church alive, the church had been nonexistent for a thousand years. Accordingly Luther wanted the Anabaptists prevented from misleading the people. Interestingly enough, he was as unwilling to approve of the death penalty as were his gentler co-workers Melanchthon and Bucer. However, by 1530, Luther, too, agreed that Anabaptists should be executed as seditious.

The Lutheran church was steadily taking shape. As we have seen, lands and cities were standing by their evangelical faith against their enemies; the theologians were standing by their teaching against the threat of false gospels. One more great task of stabilizing remained. The church life of the people needed to be strengthened.

What was the real state of affairs in the churches? To discover the answer, Elector John set up a church visitation throughout Saxony in 1527, and another, more carefully organized visitation in 1528. Armed with power to instruct and discipline, teams of theologians and lawyers summoned the pastors and leading laymen of a community and inquired into the care of church property, the moral conditions, the conduct of worship, and the teachings of church and school. Luther and Melanchthon and others who took part in the visitations were appalled and depressed at the neglect, confusion, and religious poverty they found. Church life needed to be organized anew from the ground up. It was one thing to write tracts and propose plans; getting them faithfully used was another thing.

The visitations were meant to be a temporary arrangement, a service of love on the part of the elector as a leading member of the church—an "emergency bishop" as Luther called him. Unfortunately the temporary became permanent, and thus the state church system gradually developed. Visitations were soon put into the hands of "superintendents," and then a more formal organization was set up, called a consistory, which more and more became simply a bureau of religious affairs under the prince's control. This development was not surprising. The political trend of the times was toward absolute monarchy. To say the least, Luther's sharp distinction between the spiritual and the civil realms was sadly blurred.

24. The Lutheran Church Takes Form

In the year 1529 decisive events took place in all three areas we have been discussing: politics, theological relations, and church life. Early in the year, as a result of the Saxon visitations, Luther published his two catechisms. In the preface to the *Small Catechism* he tells why. "The deplorable conditions which I recently encountered when I was a visitor moved me to prepare this brief and simple catechism. What wretchedness I beheld! The common people have no knowledge whatever of Christian teaching, and unfortunately many pastors are quite incompetent for teaching. Although the people are supposed to be Christian, are baptized, and receive the holy sacrament, they do not know the Lord's Prayer, the Creed, or the Ten Commandments, they live as if they were pigs, and now that the Gospel has been restored they have mastered the fine art of abusing liberty."

The Catechisms

Countless young people through the generations have learned the ABC's of the Christian faith from this tiny booklet. Lutherans called it the "layman's Bible." So warmly personal, so childlike, and yet so profound were Luther's explanations, that after four centuries they still nourish both the simple and the wise. Luther had no patience with people who thought they had outgrown the catechism. "I am a doctor and a preacher. Yet I do as a child who is being taught the catechism. Every morning, and whenever else I have time, I read and recite word for word the Lord's Prayer, the Ten Commandments, the Creed, the Psalms, etc. I must still read and study the catechism daily, yet I cannot master it as I wish, but must remain a child and pupil of the catechism, and I do it gladly." Not only pastors and school teachers, but also parents in the home should drill their children and their servants in it. In the Luther household Katie took her turn at reciting, too.

First, Luther urged, a child should be taught the texts of the chief parts, from the Bible and the creed, and then in simple form the meaning of the texts. Unless he knew at least this much, he should not be admitted to the Lord's Supper, for he would not know what he was coming to receive. If the child mastered the *Small Catechism,* he could be taught a richer understanding of the faith from Luther's *Large Catechism* or some other guide.

By 1529 Luther already had vast experience in teaching the elements of the faith to common people. Beginning in 1516 and frequently thereafter he had preached and written about the three traditional chief parts of instruction. As early as 1520 he published a brief explanation of all three, putting them together in his characteristic way. "Three things a man needs to know in order to be saved. First, he must know what he ought to do and ought not to do. Second, when he finds that by his own strength he can neither do the things he ought, nor leave undone the things he ought not to do, he must know *where* to seek and get the strength he needs. Third, he must know *how* to seek and get this strength." In other words: Ten Commandments, then creed, then Lord's Prayer. Already Luther had showed how the Ten Commandments unfold in a beautiful sequence: The First Table shows us our duty toward God, the Second Table our duty toward our neighbors. Already he had taught that these commandments must be understood in the light of the Golden Rule: Do to others what you wish they would do to you. "Nothing but love fulfills the commandments, and nothing but self-love breaks them." Already in dealing with the Apostles' Creed, the ordinary Christian's summary of the gospel, Luther had simplified its teaching by dividing it into three parts—Father, Son, and Holy Spirit—instead of twelve, as the medieval church had taught. Now in the catechisms of 1529 Luther refined and expanded all these insights, and added new parts masterfully explaining the Sacraments of Baptism and the Lord's Supper, and even the topic of confession for those who were about to go to Communion.

New Crises

At the time Luther was writing the catechisms, grave crises were building up for the young evangelical movement. It is astonishing that no hint of the impending battles crept into the *Small Catechism,* and surprisingly little into the *Large.* In neither did Luther even use the expression "justification by faith," though this formula had already become the watchword of his reformation. And yet the catechisms from beginning to end eloquently teach the doctrine of justification by faith without resorting to the actual term. Even in the *Large Catechism,* when Luther taught the true presence of Christ in the Lord's Supper against the Zwinglians and Anabaptists who denied it, he made no effort to explain how Christ can be present, but simply affirmed that according to the word of Scripture he is there.

While the catechisms were still on press, the political situation in Germany was growing more tense. Charles V, nearly free for the moment from his three-cornered fight with the pope and King Francis, hoped soon to deal forcefully with the religious question in Germany. This year the diet once more met at Speyer. Now the Catholic princes were strongly in the majority. They pushed through a decree stating that no further innovations should be made in Lutheran lands, nor should Catholics in them be deprived of the Mass. The Edict of Worms should still be enforced in Catholic territories, granting no liberty to Lutherans in them. Bishops and abbots should resume all their accustomed authority and revenues.

On April 19, the evangelical princes and cities read to the diet a formal protest against this decree. They must "protest and testify publicly before God that they could consent to nothing contrary to his Word." From this document came the word Protestant. What did the protest mean? Roman Catholics have often maintained that the Evangelicals were protesting *against* religious liberty for Catholics. Protestants have often regarded it as a protest *against* unfair treatment of Evangelicals. Actually the word "protest" meant something positive: to testify for their convictions. The name Protestant, incidentally, never did become popular in Germany; those who broke from Rome, especially the Lutherans and the Reformed, preferred to call themselves Evangelicals—those who follow the gospel.

The protest was significant in a still more important way. This time it was not Luther who did the testifying. Six princes and fourteen cities, who had a great deal more to lose than just their own lives, signed the protest and stood by the Reformation against the majority. Protestantism was taking form.

Charles simply ignored the protest and prepared to come to Germany personally for the next diet to settle the religious question. The Protestants pondered what course of action to take. Young Philip of Hesse had an answer. The Evangelicals should form a strong political alliance. This alliance should unite the Lutherans throughout Germany, the Swiss Zwinglians, who had extended their influence to several towns beside Zurich, and some southern German cities, such as Strassburg, which stood between the two religious viewpoints. But could these groups trust one another? After their theological feud, Luther more than ever accused Zwingli of fanaticism. Besides, hadn't Zwingli in that very year supported a war against Swiss Catholics in the name of the gospel?

Meeting at Marburg

Luther was not alone in his misgivings; some of the princes as well as the theologians agreed with him. Martin Bucer of Strassburg, however, encouraged Philip to hope that the doctrinal clash could be overcome. Philip therefore invited Luther and Zwingli and their chief colleagues to a friendly conference at Marburg. Luther agreed reluctantly. Zwingli, more politically-minded, came eagerly, declaring that he would like to be in harmony with the Wittenbergers.

For three days in October the theologians debated in Philip's handsome castle. Chalk in hand, Luther wrote on the table, "This is my body," to remind everyone where the dispute lay. Tempers were kept generally in bounds. Some misunderstandings on both sides were cleared up. In the end, however, they remained deadlocked. To the Swiss it was absurd and useless to say that Christ's body is in the sacrament, except perhaps present in our thoughts. Luther was equally adamant. When Christ promises, "I will meet you there," the whole Christ comes to us, not if we believe hard enough, but because he has promised. The real presence of Christ in the Supper fits perfectly with what we otherwise know of the ways of God. Therefore, as he wrote in his *Large Catechism*, "the whole gospel and the article of the Creed, 'I believe in the holy Christian church, the forgiveness of sins,' are embodied in this sacrament."

Even after the debate ended, Landgrave Philip tried to salvage the cause of unity. Would Luther offer a formula to which both sides might consent? He did so, but it was not acceptable. Would Luther draw up a statement expressing the measure of doctrinal harmony they had reached? The *Marburg Articles* finally satisfied both sides. On fourteen points they agreed. On the Lord's Supper, the fifteenth article, they concurred in a number of details, but the article candidly confessed that on one subject they had to differ: "Although at present we are not agreed as to whether the true body and blood are bodily present in the bread and wine, nevertheless each party should show Christian love to the other, so far as conscience can permit, and both should fervently pray Almighty God that by his Spirit he would strengthen us in the right understanding."

Because of this disagreement, Luther's party refused to consider the Zwinglians their "brothers and members of Christ," welcome at the Communion table. "Nevertheless," he wrote, "we gave them the right hand of peace and charity, agreeing that for the present harsh words and writings should cease." Luther even hoped that the last obstacle might someday be removed. At all events, however, he had come to Marburg to confess the gospel, not to negotiate with it.

In the meantime, Landgrave Philip asked, must there be full religious agreement in order to form a political alliance? It was the Lutheran governmental authorities rather than the theologians who decided that question, at a conference which met in another town while the Marburg Colloquy was taking place. In their present circumstances, when they would soon have to answer to a hostile and determined emperor, the Lutheran cities and princes insisted that religious unity would have to precede political confederation. They considered the Swiss a bad risk—a decision men still dispute warmly. One thing can be said for both the civil authorities and the theologians: With much to lose, they were asking seriously what the gospel is and what it means to confess it.

25. The Faithful Confession

A NEW showdown between the Lutherans and the emperor was to come at the Diet of Augsburg in 1530. Luther could not attend, for he was a condemned heretic and an outlaw of the empire. The responsibilities lay on other shoulders, and the outcome in God's hands.

External events eased some of the pressure on the Lutherans. Though the emperor was at peace with both the pope and France, everyone knew that the alliance was shaky. The Turks had advanced so far up the Danube in 1529 that they had besieged Vienna — although unsuccessfully. Charles had to have a united Germany in order to protect the southeastern flank of the empire. Perhaps the Lutherans could hold the Turkish threat over the emperor in order to win concessions. Whatever the outcome, however, for Luther disobedience or even indifference on this score was unthinkable. The emperor was still the Protestants' overlord and God's annointed. Luther wrote in 1529 that it was their duty to support Charles' projected war against the Turkish invaders.

At any rate the Lutheran powers hoped for an open discussion of the religious question at the diet. They commissioned Philipp Melanchthon to draw up a confession of their faith, to show that they were not brash innovators but heirs of the ancient faith of the church, entitled to good standing within the Christian empire. Charles, though wishing for a more conciliatory policy from Rome, was determined to keep the empire united and Catholic.

At Coburg Castle

In April Luther proceeded with his theological colleagues as far as the Coburg Castle, on the edge of the Saxon domains. The others went on to the diet. For nearly six months Luther remained at the Coburg while the destiny of the church was being decided 150 miles away, four days' distance by courier. These months open to us an incomparable insight into the man and his faith.

He chafed and fretted, worrying with good reason that Melanchthon might concede too much to their adversaries. At the same time Luther wrote effective letters to strengthen the faith and courage of his co-workers at the diet. Again, as at the Wartburg nine years earlier, he busied himself with writing, including subjects ranging from the Bible to current topics to Aesop's fables. Sickness plagued him. Increasingly his ailments were taking their toll—painful kidney stones, chronic stomach troubles, attacks of nervous exhaustion, and other ills. This time he had spells of dizziness and "a ringing or rather thundering" in his ears. Then in June he received news that his father was dead. He took his Psalter into his room and mourned for two days. Then he went back to work. His old spiritual assaults hounded him in his solitude. On one occasion, he wrote to Melanchthon, "Satan conquered me so far that he forced me to leave my room and seek the company of other men."

In spite of all the pressure upon him, about twenty writings from his pen witness to his remarkable vigor, and a stream of wonderful letters displays the strength of his colorful personality. A buoyant sense of humor, a frank exhilaration over the everyday wonders of God's nature, an affectionate whimsy in his family letters, all nourished by his sturdy faith, now strengthened his faith in turn.

To his household in Wittenberg: "There is a grove directly under our windows here where the jackdaws and crows are holding a diet. They fly to and fro so fast and make such a racket day and night that they all seem drunk and silly. I wonder how their breath holds out, they bicker so. They care not for a palace to meet in, for their hall is roofed with the vault of the sky, its floor is the carpet of green grass, and its walls are as distant as the ends of the world. They do not ask for horses and trappings, for they have winged chariots to escape man's wrath. As far as I can gather from an interpreter, they are planning a mighty campaign against wheat, barley, oats, and all kinds of grain, a war in which many a knight will do great deeds."

To the chancellor of Saxony during the darkest days of the diet, in order to strengthen the hearts of the diplomats under *their* pressures: "Recently I saw two miracles. First, as I looked out of my window, I saw the stars and the sky and the whole vault of heaven, with no pillars to support it. And yet the sky did not fall and the vault remained secure. But there are some who want to see the pillars and would like to clasp and feel them, else they fidget and tremble. If they could only feel and see the pillars, they would be satisfied that the sky will remain secure. Again, I saw great, thick clouds roll above us, so heavy that they looked like great seas, and I saw no ground on which they could rest nor any barrels to hold them. And yet they did not fall on us, but threatened us and floated on. When they had passed by, there appeared a shining rainbow which was the floor that held them up. It is such a weak, thin little floor that it was almost lost in the clouds and looked more like a ray coming through a stained glass window than a strong floor, so that it was as marvelous as the weight of the clouds. But some people look at the thickness of the clouds and the thinness of the ray, and they fear and worry. They would like to feel how strong the rainbow is, and when they cannot, they think the clouds will bring on another flood."

To his four-year-old son Hans: "I know a lovely garden where many children in golden jackets gather rosy apples under the trees, and pears and cherries and plums. They sing and skip and have a merry time. And they have fine ponies with golden bridles and silver saddles. I asked the gardener who these children were. He said, 'They are the children who say their prayers and learn and are good.' And I said, 'Good man, I too have a son, and his name is Hans Luther. May he come into the garden, too, and eat the rosy apples and pears and ride a fine pony and play with these children?' The man said, 'If he says his prayers and is good, he may come into the garden, and Phil and Justy too [the sons of Melanchthon and Jonas], and they shall all have whistles and drums, and shoot little silver crossbows.' God bless you. Give Auntie Lena my love and a kiss from me. Your loving father, MARTIN LUTHER."

The Augsburg Confession

It was at Augsburg, however, that the public confessing took place, and this required courage and wisdom. The Evangelicals were determined to defend their cause. In June, when crowds gathered to greet the emperor's arrival and knelt to receive a papal blessing from the cardinal legate, Elector John and Landgrave Philip remained stiffly erect. When the emperor demanded that all the princes march in the Corpus Christi festival procession, old Margrave George of Brandenburg knelt before him and bared his neck: "Before I let anyone take from me the Word of God and ask me to deny my God, I will kneel and let him strike off my head!" The procession was attended only by the Catholic dignitaries and scarcely a hundred citizens of Augsburg.

Melanchthon had already been at work on the Lutherans' confession. When Luther read it in May, he remarked, "I like it very much, and I see nothing to alter or improve in it. Indeed, I could not do so if I tried, for I cannot tread so softly and gently." Melanchthon, however, continued to polish it. The Roman Catholic legate and Eck, meanwhile, were busy trying to rouse hostility against the Evangelicals, to silence their preachers, and to prevent a hearing of their position. Eck prepared 404 theses listing errors and innovations of Luther, Zwingli, Carlstadt, and others, to imply that their heresies were all of one piece.

Finally, in a closed session of the diet on June 25, two chancellors of Saxony read the entire *Augsburg Confession* in Latin and German. Luther was jubilant when he heard the report. To him the event fulfilled the words of Psalm 119:46: "I will also speak of thy testimonies before kings, and shall not be put to shame." "I am overjoyed to be living at this hour, when Christ is openly confessed by so many in a great public assembly and with so good a confession," he wrote. "Our enemies thought they had gained a great point by having the emperor forbid our preaching, but the dupes did not realize that by our written confession this doctrine is spread more widely than it could have been by ten preachers." Luther was right. Deeply impressed by the confession, five cities immediately added their signatures to those of the original seven princes and two cities. More cities soon followed.

Great wisdom and courage were still needed. In August the Roman Catholics read a confutation, prepared chiefly by Eck, as their reply to the Lutheran confession. The emperor and some Catholic princes tried threats. A moderate party of Catholics tried to draw Melanchthon into further concessions. Luther urged him not to yield an inch. In the end both princes and theologians stood firm. Finally in September the diet voted that the *Augsburg Confession* had been refuted, and that the Protestants were bound to recant. The emperor gave them until April 15 to submit. "Let us believe that Christ is yet strong enough to rule all fools and babblers who condemn him," wrote Luther. "If war comes, let it come; we have prayed and done enough."

26. The Continuing Struggle

MELANCHTHON wrote the *Augsburg Confession*. Princes and free city councils signed it before the imperial diet. But this did not mean that they had taken Luther's place, that he was no longer needed. He was needed, and although he was weary and ill, he had no intention of leaving his post before receiving a clear sign that he had been relieved of it. As the Reformation moved into a period of unprecedented expansion during this decade, Luther's counsel was sought repeatedly by great and small in public and private matters, and he remained as vigorously productive as ever. The Lutheran church, officially illegal, would continue to struggle on. Luther would continue to struggle on in its behalf.

Politics and Problems

The trend in Germany ran strongly toward the Reformation. The great seaport city of Lübeck was an example. While the diet was still in session in 1530, the city had accepted the Lutheran faith. The citizens refused to have any but evangelical preachers, and asked Bugenhagen to come and help them reorganize the church. When the emperor issued a mandate forbidding changes in church practices there, they ignored it.

Threatened with force by the Edict of Augsburg, the Evangelicals formed a political alliance, the Smalcald League. By the middle of the decade it was one of the great powers of Europe. City after city, and several states, espoused the Reformation and joined the league. Even England and France courted the league's favor, and a papal legate, Vergerio, came to Wittenberg in 1535 to talk with Luther about calling a church council. The emperor could not stem the tide because he was kept busy by the Turks and by two more wars with King Francis of France.

Meanwhile, supporting the gospel of Christ by means of political and military force caused the Evangelicals grave problems and great misgivings. Both Melanchthon's *Augsburg Confession* and Chancellor Brueck's judicious preface to it had insisted that the Lutheran churches belong in the continuity of the ancient church. Even Charles' summons to the diet had called upon all parties to hear one another's beliefs charitably, in order "to have all of us embrace a single, true religion and live together in unity and in one fellowship and church, even as we are all enlisted under one Christ." But in the light of the diet's decree, how could the Smalcald League prove that it was not deliberately establishing a new, separatist church?

There was another serious question: Would princes and cities be justified to resist their overlord, the emperor, with force? Luther had said no, unless the overlord commanded his subjects clearly to disobey God; otherwise they must suffer patiently or emigrate. The Protestant jurists, however, argued that according to the imperial constitution, the princes were not simply subjects, but co-rulers with responsibility for the empire. Luther allowed himself to be convinced that "the sovereign power itself is subject to the law."

Still another problem: The Swiss and a cluster of four southern German cities, dissatisfied with the Lutheran confession at the diet, had drawn up statements of their own. Neither was received by the emperor. Although the Swiss remained independent and aloof, the southern German cities joined the Smalcald League. This made religious agreement urgent, since no one dreamed of political unity without church unity.

The Strassburg reformer, Martin Bucer, was the man who most keenly felt the need for a united religious front. He worked industriously to bring together the southern Germans and the Wittenbergers. The stumbling block was still the doctrine of the Lord's Supper. Finally Bucer convinced the Lutherans of his sincerity and soundness. In 1536, with Luther's approval, both parties signed the *Wittenberg Concord* with heartfelt thanksgiving to God and with a joyful Communion service. Then they submitted it to the southern German cities for their acceptance. Some variations of outlook remained—the seeds of later arguments—but for the time being the German Evangelicals received one another as brothers in Christ.

Part of the price for this unity was to ignore the Swiss Zwinglians and to denounce the Anabaptists. By 1536, however, a new star was rising on the Swiss horizon. At the age of twenty-seven, John Calvin, at Geneva, was giving shape and leadership to Reformed Christianity. He won the warm friendship of Bucer and Melanchthon.

No such hopes, meanwhile, arose over the Anabaptists. General distrust of them was only confirmed about this time by the fantastic episode at Münster in northwestern Germany, where an Anabaptist sect seized the city and established there the "heavenly Jerusalem." Its director, calling himself King David, introduced polygamy under the guidance of heavenly visions. In 1535 this grotesque kingdom was wiped out with great cruelty by the joint armies of the Catholic bishop and the Lutheran Philip of Hesse. Most other Anabaptists, horrified by the excesses at Münster, tried to rebuild their movement on a peaceful basis. But Lutherans, like their Catholic and Reformed neighbors, continued to persecute them all. Occasionally Luther tried to distinguish between those Anabaptists who were just "in error" and those who were also seditious and therefore deserved strict punishment, but his record on toleration is not very impressive by modern standards.

The German Bible

The year 1534 saw one of Luther's supreme achievements, the publication of the entire German Bible. It has been called his greatest monument. Luther could not know that it would prove to be the greatest single influence in shaping the modern German language out of the confusion of medieval dialects. He could not know that even into the present day Germans would speak of the Scriptures in their own tongue as the "Luther translation." Its place in German culture is even higher than that which the King James Version occupies in ours. All this is of secondary importance, however. Luther's German Bible is his supreme achievement because it fulfilled his supreme desire. This was to place the Word of God into the hands of the people, for here was where they would find Jesus Christ. "The holy scripture is the cradle in which Christ is laid," Luther felt.

Luther wisely did not try to translate the Bible all by himself. He realized that he needed the best help he could get. Shortly after returning from the Wartburg, he formed a committee of expert scholars which usually met once a week. They worked not only on the Old Testament but also on the New, and continued to revise and improve their translation as long as Luther lived. While he profited greatly from the experts' help, Luther with good reason kept the reins of the committee in his own hands. Two great tasks needed to be accomplished, and no one else came near to Luther's genius in bringing the two into harmony. One was accuracy in discovering what the words of Scripture really mean. The other was the art of expressing those meanings so that all the divine majesty and the human verve of the Bible would come through to the common people.

Luther tells us what a strenuous task this was. "Good heavens, how hard it is to make the Hebrew prophets speak German! They resist giving up their native tongue for a barbarous idiom, just as the nightingale would not change her sweet song to imitate the cuckoo." "To translate properly is to turn the spirit of a foreign language into our own idiom." "To express the idea in German one must ask the mother in the home, the children in the street, and the common man in the market place. Then people will recognize that someone is speaking to them in German." Luther visited the slaughterhouse to learn how to describe the parts of animals mentioned in Moses' laws on sacrifice. To learn the names of the precious stones mentioned in the vision of heaven in Revelation, he visited the elector's collection of jewels.

Luther furnished the books of the Bible with helpful prefaces, but otherwise let Scripture speak for itself, unlike the Roman Catholic Bibles, which were peppered with officially approved "glosses"

or explanations of various passages. In his 1522 preface to the New Testament he commented that the best of the twenty-seven books were John's Gospel and Paul's Epistles, especially Romans. Every Christian ought to read them "first and most frequently, and by daily reading make them as familiar as his daily bread." His reason was that these books show us most clearly what the wondrous gift of the gospel is, and the relation of faith and love. On another occasion, however, he remarked that for the common man and for young people, the first three Gospels are best. In the Old Testament he particularly loved the Psalms, which he called "a Bible in miniature," since it "tells not only the works of the saints, but also how they speak with God and pray."

The Smalcald Articles

In 1534 a very different kind of pope came to Peter's throne. Paul III realized that the Lutheran advances could be arrested only if a drastic housecleaning took place within the Roman Catholic church. He determined to call a general church council—something that Charles V had often urged earlier. Part of Vergerio's mission in Germany was to find out if the Smalcald League and Luther would send delegates. Meeting at Smalcald, the Lutheran powers laid down several conditions: (1) it must be a free Christian council, not a rigged papal council; (2) it must admit laymen and not treat the Lutherans in advance as heretics; (3) the standard of judgment must be the Bible, not the pope; (4) the council ought to meet on German soil. These conditions, of course, were altogether unacceptable to Rome.

The league, in any case, wanted to be prepared with a positive statement of faith. Luther was asked by the new elector of Saxony to prepare one. John Frederick the Great-Hearted, twenty-nine years old when he succeeded his father, John, in 1532, had grown up as a convinced Lutheran under the guidance of Spalatin. He was pleased with the vigorous *Smalcald Articles* which Luther drafted late in 1536. Luther did not expect to live long, and since he had never been quite satisfied with the mild tone of Melanchthon's *Apology* (defense) *of the Augsburg Confession* he wanted to deliver a kind of last will and testament to show exactly where he stood.

Part I of the *Smalcald Articles* acknowledged that no conflict existed between Lutherans and Roman Catholics over the ancient dogmas of the Trinity and the person of Christ. Part II insisted, however, that the doctrine of justification by faith in Christ alone is the article on which "rests all that we teach and practice." "Nothing in this article can be given up or compromised." This doctrine, Luther held, utterly demolished the Roman Catholic view of the Mass and all its "brood of vermin and poison of idolatries." He meant Catholic church practices and also the view of the papacy. Finally, Part III tersely listed important teachings and practices which could profitably be discussed in a council or even informally.

The *Articles* were presented for adoption at a meeting of the Smalcald League in February, 1537, which Luther was too ill to attend. But they were not adopted. Melanchthon pressed for a milder statement, and the diplomats accepted his advice. Nevertheless the *Smalcald Articles* were signed by a number of clergymen gathered at Smalcald and soon came to be recognized as a high expression of Lutheran teaching. They represented the final declaration of Lutheran independence from the Roman Catholic church.

In the preface of the *Smalcald Articles,* Luther referred to the rumor that the pope intended to call a council. "I don't believe it," Luther said in effect, "he wouldn't dare!" This was not quite true, but Pope Paul found that the times were far from ripe for a Catholic council. Many churchmen, rulers, and even the emperor obstructed the pope's intention. Not until 1545 did the great council of Trent begin. When it did, it represented not Western Christendom, but only the Roman Catholic fragment of it.

Expansion

Protestantism continued to expand. "Wait a little," Luther had said early in the 1530's. "Who knows what God will do even before ten years have gone by?" Sweden and Denmark became strongly Lutheran. When the elector of Brandenburg and Duke George of Saxony died, the successors of these powerful Catholic princes declared their lands Lutheran in 1539. Luther preached in the same castle where, twenty years earlier, he had debated with John Eck in the presence of Duke George.

In the early 1540's the elector archbishop of Cologne and several bishops considered becoming Protestant. Meanwhile Henry VIII of England, if not actually turning his country Protestant, at least had cut it loose from Rome in 1534. Important individuals were switching their faith, such as Bernardino Ochino, the general of a monastic order and the outstanding preacher in Italy.

With the emperor's blessing, three conferences in 1540–41 between Protestant and Roman Catholic theologians and laymen attempted to settle the difference between the faiths by arbitration. Bucer, Melanchthon, and Calvin were among the Protestant representatives; two cardinals and John Eck among the Catholics. Luther expected little success from these efforts to reconcile such deep-seated differences.

Troubles

No one will ever know whether or not Luther's judgment was right. Unfortunately, this was just the time when fateful Protestant weaknesses appeared and Roman Catholic strength revived. Honest differences in the interpretation of the gospel as well as personal rivalries arose among Lutherans. The split widened between the Lutherans and Reformed. At the same time, follies and clashing ambitions among Lutheran rulers wrecked the Smalcald League. Chief among the latter calamities were the bigamy of Philip of Hesse and the ruthless ambition of Duke Maurice of Saxony. Both situations brought grief to the Protestant cause.

Landgrave Philip, married young to a wife he did not like, had long been unfaithful to her. Unlike many princes of the day, he developed a sensitive conscience over his infidelity. If he could have a wife for whom he had genuine affection, he thought, he could keep his marriage vow. But what about his present wife? Three solutions lay at hand. If he were Catholic, the pope could find some way to annul the marriage; but Philip was no Catholic. Second, there was divorce. Third, bigamy. The third alternative was not impossible. Interpreting the Bible rigidly, the medieval church had forbidden divorce, but in rare instances winked at bigamy, since the Old Testament permitted it and the New Testament never actually forbade it. Bucer, Luther, and Melanchthon took this position when Philip consulted them in 1539. Luther had given the same judgment almost a decade earlier when Henry VIII of England had approached him over the question of divorcing his queen. Philip proceeded to plan a wedding to a seventeen-year-old girl, having obtained the written consent of his first wife.

The three theologians' approval had been given, reluctantly, on condition that the marriage be kept secret. But, of course, the secret was soon out, and a great scandal broke upon both Philip and the theologians. Luther refused to collapse over the embarrassment. He deeply regretted the scandal, but "where no earthly law nor wisdom" could help, he had given private "confessional counsel." This latter, he felt, must be kept private and undisclosed even if a lie should be necessary to protect it. In this, Luther yielded neither to Philip's anger nor to public abuse. Philip was forced to go to Emperor Charles to seek his pardon. The allies of the Smalcald League took great offense at the incident, and popular opinion still regards it as the darkest blot on Luther's career.

Meanwhile Maurice of Saxony, on becoming duke in 1541 at the age of twenty, immediately embarked on a career of unscrupulous ambition. The story of his astonishing role, first in betraying the Reformation and then in saving it, will be told in Chapter 28.

Small wonder that the aging Luther wrote to Melanchthon, "They will say in Rome that we are coming to blows and that we will uproot our own teaching. But God will do what is right."

27. The Aging Luther

THE fire in Luther's spirit continued to burn brightly even though he was tired and ill. He kept up his phenomenal productivity in the press and at the university. The literary output of his last fifteen years almost equalled that of the preceding twenty. From the last year of his life we have nearly a dozen publications plus lectures and sermons and over seventy letters.

His judgment—sometimes wise and sometimes not—remained important to all sorts of people on all sorts of matters. As long as he lived the strength of his personality helped to hold together factions which later would split apart in bitterness.

Tenderness

His *Table Talk* and his letters show that he never lost his flashing sense of humor and his tenderness toward the people he loved. "Katie, you have a husband who loves you; many an empress is not so well off." "George Karg has taken a rich wife and sold his freedom. I am luckier. When Katie gets saucy she gets nothing but a box on the ear." In a letter of 1540 he saluted his industrious wife: "To my beloved wife Katherine, Mrs. Dr. Luther, mistress of the pig market [which was near Katie's garden], Lady von Zulsdorf [where she had a farm], and whatever other titles may befit your Grace."

He took great delight in his children and spent much time with them. At Christmas, 1534, he wrote the charming carol, "From Heaven Above," probably for his own children to sing and act out as a manger pageant.

In September, 1542, Luther's thirteen-year-old daughter, his lovely Magdalena, lay on her deathbed. "Little Lena," he said to her, "you would like to stay with your father here, and you would also be glad to go to your Father in heaven, wouldn't you?" "Yes, dear father," she answered. "As God wills." She died in his arms. He chided himself: "In a thousand years no bishop has been so blessed by God as I have been. Why can't my heart be happy and thankful now?" But he comforted his grief: "I have sent a living saint to heaven." That Christmas he wrote another carol, sturdy in faith:

What harm can sin and death now do?
You have the one true God with you!

Irascibility

If only these features were the main theme of Luther's later years! Unfortunately, we find him increasingly irritable, coarse, and bitter. He wrote caustic and intolerant attacks against the Jews and against "fanatics" of all kinds, and savage volleys against his enemies on the side of Rome. No doubt we may make allowances. His illnesses were partly responsible for his violence. Further, many of his adversaries had given him exactly the same treatment; he lived in a coarse, crude age. His bark was worse than his bite; this was one way he worked off steam. But our judgment inevitably remains that all too often Luther loosened the reins and indulged his temper far more than he ought, and that his own best friends were often embarrassed by these outbursts.

Time and again Luther had urged men to be patient in awaiting outward results from the preaching of the gospel, and patient with the seedlings that grew from its sowing. In his aging years, however, like many men, he felt that he saw signs that the world was approaching its end in wickedness. He feared that the dikes were about to burst over his movement. War was ready to break out in Germany. He felt bitterly disappointed with the people, high and low alike, for their ingratitude to God and the carelessness of their lives.

In the summer of 1545, while on a journey, he became so depressed—for one reason, over the frivolity and waywardness of the young people in Wittenberg—that he wrote his wife, "I am tired of that city, and do not wish to return. I will wander around here and eat the bread of charity before I will martyr and soil my poor old last days with the disorderly life of Wittenberg, where all my painful and costly work goes for nothing." He wanted Katie to sell the property and move to Zulsdorf. The news created consternation in Wittenberg. The town sent its burgomaster to him, the university sent Melanchthon and Bugenhagen, the elector sent his physician. Together they persuaded the old man to return.

However, the old courage, the old faithfulness, the old fire flamed forth again. Luther took up his work once more, but he knew that his end was near. In November he finished his great series of lectures on Genesis: "God grant that others after me do a better job with it. I can do no more, I am weak. Pray God to give me a good, blessed departure."

But one more duty called. His friends, the two counts of Mansfeld, had fallen into a quarrel over their property. They asked Luther to mediate between them. In the dead of winter, when travel was unsafe, Luther journeyed to Eisleben to offer his help. When Katie learned that Luther had taken ill on the way, she became anxious. Her husband chided her. "Unless you stop worrying," he wrote, "I am afraid the earth will swallow me up or the elements will persecute me. Don't you know the catechism and the creed? Pray, and let God handle the matter, as it says in Psalm 55: 'Cast your burden on the LORD, and he will sustain you.'"

That was on February 10, 1546. A week later the quarrel was settled and the counts signed an agreement. That same day Luther felt desperately ill. Jonas and other friends, two of his sons, and two physicians attended him. Shortly after midnight, on February 18, he commended himself to God's hands in prayer, and recited John 3:16, "God so loved the world. . . ." He suffered a stroke. Jonas had to speak loudly to make him hear: "Reverend father, will you stand by Christ and the doctrine you have preached?" The dying man rallied his strength and said a distinct "Yes!"

Then it was all over. Martin Luther died in the very village where he had been born sixty-two years before.

28. Coda

PROFESSOR Melanchthon interrupted the lecture at the Wittenberg University when the news of Luther's death arrived. "Gone is the charioteer and the chariot of Israel [his allusion was to the prophet Elijah, 2 Kings 2:12], who guided the church in the last age of the world," he announced to his audience. He offered a prayer: "O Son of God, thou Immanuel crucified and risen for us, I pray thee to guide, preserve, and protect thy church."

Burial

As Luther's body was brought back to Wittenberg, at many places weeping people lined the road. Melanchthon, though no sentimentalist, spoke for countless common folk as well as Luther's intimate co-workers: "We are like orphans who have had a dear, wonderful man for a father, and now have had him taken away from us." Through the north door of the Castle Church entered the funeral procession. The body was interred under the floor of the church near the pulpit where Luther had so often opened the Word of God to the people.

"Before two years are past," Dr. Jonas declared at the first memorial service in Eisleben, "we shall realize, and so will the papists, that Dr. Martin Luther has left a mighty power behind him."

War

He was right. War clouds were gathering. The Roman Catholic church was already busy at the Council of Trent cleaning its house and sharply defining its doctrine against the heretics. Emperor Charles, having defeated Francis in 1544 for the fourth time, was ready to use force on the Protestants. The Smalcald League was paralyzed, with Philip of Hesse halfway under the emperor's thumb after the bigamy affair, and Maurice of Saxony eagerly looking for a way to take electoral Saxony away from his cousin John Frederick.

In July, 1546, Charles struck. He was determined to redeem his promise to keep the empire Catholic. The pope sent his blessing for this attack upon "the enemies of God," and offered indulgences to those who would support Charles in this Smalcald War. The Protestants fought ineptly. Philip of Hesse dragged his feet. The unscrupulous Duke Maurice made a deal with the emperor and launched an attack upon Elector John Frederick, the Protestant leader. In April, 1547, the elector was defeated and captured. Philip was persuaded to give himself up. Charles kept both princes prisoner. The victorious emperor entered the Castle Church in Wittenberg and gazed at the arch-heretic's grave. He refused to give an order to tear it open and desecrate it, however, for he respected his adversary.

Luther was dead only one year and already all Germany lay at Charles' mercy.

The Tide Turns

Then a strange thing happened. Charles discovered that he could not stamp out the evangelical faith. The most he could impose upon the Protestants was a temporary compromise, the Augsburg Interim. Melanchthon and others bowed to it, and some leaders, such as Bucer, left the country. But other Protestant leaders and princes defied and denounced it, and the common people raised a massive resistance against it. Earlier, Luther had lost his faith in "Mr. Everyman." Now the people proved him wrong.

Suddenly, in 1552, Maurice switched his politics, raised an army, and drove the emperor out of Germany. Charles barely escaped capture. The tide was turned.

In 1555 came a decisive event in the history of Europe, the Peace of Augsburg. It acknowledged that Protestants and Catholics would have to agree to disagree. It formally ratified the principle, generally in operation since the 1520's, that each government would decide which faith would be officially recognized. Dissenters should be free to move elsewhere.

This may seem a very limited advance toward religious liberty, but it was the first definite step. Lutheranism was now a legal faith. The next year Emperor Charles, admitting that he had been unable to make good his pledge to keep the empire Catholic, abdicated the imperial throne.

A Song and a Faith

> A mighty fortress is our God,
> A bulwark never failing. . . .

Luther had composed this "battle hymn of the Reformation" in 1527, a year of conflict and uncertainty, the year of his own most bitter spiritual assaults. Now, after his death, its prophetic message continued more than ever to summon and strengthen men.

Back of the song stood the faith that Luther had preached, whose principles of action have been described thus: "Do not rely on men but trust in God. Do not fear men but fear God."

In faithfulness and failure, in service and selfishness, in decline and renewal, Christendom still marches on. Whenever it needs to be recalled to genuine faith, Luther lives. Pastor Frederick Myconius' letter to the elector of Saxony after Luther's funeral was prophetic. "This Dr. Luther will not and cannot die. Only now will he really live." Myconius was only echoing the thought which Luther, without the slightest boastfulness, had chosen for a motto long before, in the midst of his struggles. Cooped up in Coburg Castle, Luther had written on the walls of his room the words of Psalm 118:17—"I shall not die, but I shall live, and recount the deeds of the Lord."

PART FIVE

The Man Who Sought God

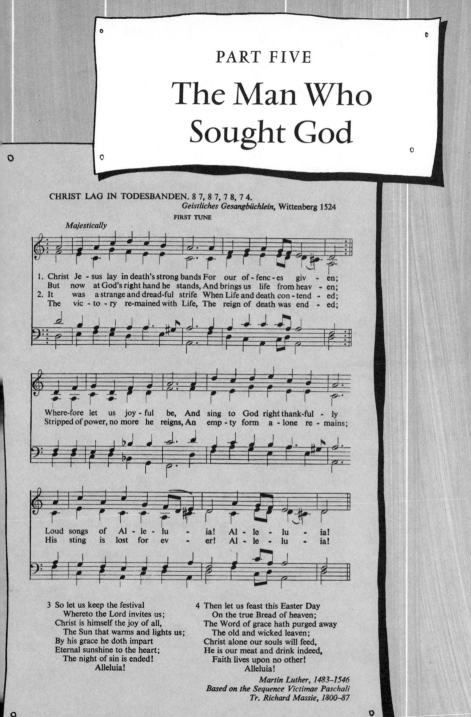

CHRIST LAG IN TODESBANDEN. 8 7, 8 7, 7 8, 7 4.

Geistliches Gesangbüchlein, Wittenberg 1524

FIRST TUNE

Majestically

1. Christ Je - sus lay in death's strong bands For our of - fenc - es giv - en;
But now at God's right hand he stands, And brings us life from heav - en;
2. It was a strange and dread-ful strife When Life and death con - tend - ed;
The vic - to - ry re-mained with Life, The reign of death was end - ed;

Where-fore let us joy - ful be, And sing to God right thank-ful - ly
Stripped of power, no more he reigns, An emp - ty form a - lone re - mains;

Loud songs of Al - le - lu - ia! Al - le - lu - ia!
His sting is lost for ev - er! Al - le - lu - ia!

3 So let us keep the festival
　Whereto the Lord invites us;
Christ is himself the joy of all,
　The Sun that warms and lights us;
By his grace he doth impart
Eternal sunshine to the heart;
　The night of sin is ended!
　　Alleluia!

4 Then let us feast this Easter Day
　On the true Bread of heaven;
The Word of grace hath purged away
　The old and wicked leaven;
Christ alone our souls will feed,
He is our meat and drink indeed,
　Faith lives upon no other!
　　Alleluia!

Martin Luther, 1483–1546
Based on the Sequence Victimae Paschali
Tr. Richard Massie, 1800–87

29. What Kind of Man?

How can you take the measure of this man, Martin Luther?

There are many standards of judgment which you could apply to him. You might ask his contemporaries what kind of person Luther was and tally their judgments pro and con. Those who dealt intimately with him, friends and enemies, should have the freshest and most colorful insights to help you evaluate Luther's character and personal qualities. On the other hand you might turn to later observers for their opinions. These should have the advantage of clearer perspective in judging Luther. However, this is not necessarily the case. The perspective may be hazy if the observer does not know Luther and his times accurately enough; it may be blurred if he reads the records through the eyeglasses of prejudice.

Again, you can ask not merely who Luther was, but also what he did. What did he accomplish? How was Europe different at the time Luther died from what it was when he became a fledgling professor—and to what extent was Luther the author of the change? Furthermore, what has been his impact on history down to our own tempestuous times?

You can test his purposes and intentions in the light of his actual performance—and vice versa. Luther tried to renew the church of his day. How do his insights and efforts and actual results compare with those of other men who also sincerely sought the renewal of the church—Erasmus, Zwingli, Calvin, Müntzer, the gentler Anabaptists, the Englishman Thomas Cranmer, the Roman Catholics who remained loyal to the papacy and finally produced the reforming Council of Trent?

You can examine Luther's own understanding of himself and his work. Was he realistic in his judgment or not?

Two striking passages which Luther wrote during the hottest, most critical period of his battle may furnish a good springboard for an effort to evaluate him.

1520. "As for the slanders and evil names with which my person is attacked, they do not trouble me. It has never been my intention to get even with those who slander my person, my life, my work, my character. That I am not worthy of praise, I myself know perfectly well. But I will let no man reproach me that in defending the scriptures I am more pointed and impetuous than some seem to like, neither will I be silent. Whoever will, let him freely scold, slander, and condemn my person and my life—he is already forgiven. But let no one expect from me either favor or patience who would make liars of my Lord Christ, whom I preach, and the Holy Spirit. I am nothing at all, but for the Word of Christ I will give answer with a glad heart and a bold mind, and without partiality. To this end God has given me a cheerful and fearless spirit, which my enemies will not embitter, I trust, not in all eternity."

1522. "I ask that men call themselves not Lutherans but Christians. Who is this Luther? My teaching is not my own, nor have I been crucified for anyone. Why should it happen to me, miserable, stinking bag of worms that I am, that the children of Christ should be called by my insignificant name? I am not anybody's master, nor do I wish to be. With the one church I have in common the teaching of Christ who alone is our master."

How many other figures of history can you name who wielded as great an influence upon their own time as Martin Luther, and who have remained influential through generation after generation? Of those whom you have listed, how many owed their opportunity for fame to birth, wealth, or to the ambitious climb to positions of power? And what were the tools and the techniques by which they exerted their influence over others? These questions may serve as a frame of comparison and contrast for a portrait of Luther.

The portrait you draw may be a tentative sketch if you are not yet a master of the subject. In any case the picture can scarcely be dull. Luther is too full of lights and shadows, of strengths and blind spots and weaknesses.

A Bold Man

"Pointed and impetuous." Surely the most obvious quality about Luther is his boldness. Bold he was in blazing his uncharted way through the unsatisfying system of the medieval church until he attained his insight into the gospel. If all he had sought was "peace of mind," he would have welcomed indulgences and the church's security, not fought them. Incredibly bold he was when this new insight required him to resist and then attack the entrenched authority of the church. In many respects the Middle Ages were less tightly regimented than they are often portrayed. But when it came to the requirement of obedience to the church system itself, there was no room for challenge. Luther did not shrink, but made room for the challenge.

This meant for him a lifetime of controversy. "Slanders and evil names" and solid opposition assailed him from without. From within came all the battles involved in the task of rebuilding church life on an evangelical basis. Would you say that Luther spoiled for fights? In any case he unhesitatingly accepted the controversies that came, however bitter and difficult they might be, applying to himself the old proverb, "To split a tough log you need a tough wedge." After all, these controversies were the outward counterpart of the "assaults" which he had to combat within his own soul. If he must battle to bring himself into trustful obedience to Jesus Christ, his Lord, he could also meet the attacks which came from men. Both were life-time struggles, not a victory followed by living "happily ever after."

Will you call this boldness courage—or merely blind stubborn-ness or sheer perversity? Here the judgments will differ, for we usually reserve the word "courage" to describe a boldness which in some sense serves a worthy end. For example, if you hold that Luther was only rebelling from the true church of Christ, the better word for his daring would be "perversity." Luther himself was con-vinced that his sharpness and impetuosity had one goal alone: the defense of the gospel, the sovereign good news about Christ. Or is it possible that courage and perversity and stubbornness may coexist in varying combinations in the same person! In any case, Luther's bold-ness bore the marks of rugged integrity, blunt honesty, and an utter absence of pretense.

An Angry Man

What of his anger and his quick temper? Like his crudeness, these aspects of his temperament cannot be written off by saying that he was a colorful personality or by using other excuses. They are an inescapable, enduring part of the picture. "If only Luther would keep quiet!" sighed Melanchthon as early as the mid-1520's. During the reformer's early years he commented, "I had hoped that with age he would grow milder, but in fact, all this opposition irritates him and makes him more violent." If we are to understand and evaluate his anger, it is important to examine the occasions and targets of his outbursts. Generally they have to do directly with the "cause of the gospel" as he understood it. Moreover he realized at times that his temper had flown out of bounds. On the one hand he could protest that his enemies drove him to be vehement: "They shouldn't bait the dog!" On the other hand he could envy a more even temper: "I am the rough woodman who has to cut a path, but Philipp goes along it quietly and peacefully, builds and plants, sows and waters, at his pleasure." Still, he maintained that bluntness and openness have advantages. In contrast to Erasmus's urbane and reserved approach to the reform of the church, which Luther called "walking on eggs," Luther declared, "I like my frankness better." And against the sniping of his early opponent: "An open attack is better than a bite from under cover."

A Vital and Affectionate Man

Anger was only one feature of Luther's temperament. It had another side, a more solid and stable one. He had enormous vitality and a genius for harnessing his energy to do effective work, even in the face of pressure and illness. Further, he was honest in disclaiming any personal rancor against his attackers. He had a "glad and cheerful spirit" which ran deeper than his assaults of melancholy and an inner serenity which came from his willingness to leave his cause in God's hands. As he wrote to Melanchthon during the agonizing days of the Diet of Augsburg: "If our cause is false, let us back down; but if it is true, why should we make a liar of God who gives us such great promises?"

We have already seen other sound and attractive features of Luther's character. Which would you consider most worthy of mention, besides his affectionate tenderness in his home life, his generosity, his robust humor, his love of nature and of music? No repressed and joyless bluenose, Luther was able to relax and have a good time. Once he wrote to the Prince of Anhalt: "I thought Your Grace might be so timid as to consider it a sin to be happy, as I have often thought and still do at times. It is true that joy in sin is the devil, but joy with good, upright people, in the fear of God and with moderation, pleases him. Your Grace should be happy in all things, inwardly in Christ and outwardly in God's gifts, for he gives them to us that we may have pleasure in them and thank him for them." With young university students Luther was far more patient and understanding than Melanchthon; with countless persons of high or humble station who turned to him as a personal guide, he was thoughtful and helpful.

An Unambitious Man

As for himself, Luther was singularly unambitious for personal power. "I am not anybody's master, nor do I wish to be: Christ alone is our master." Luther maintained this attitude consistently throughout his life. His forceful personality influenced men deeply. Like Lincoln he was equally at ease with the great and the lowly. He inspired intense loyalty among many in both groups—though he alienated others. He was often brusque and opinionated. But never did he make his own will the decisive factor in moving men to his judgments. Thus the sneer of his enemies, "pope of Wittenberg," missed its target. He did not dictate the church's beliefs; he submitted them to Scripture. Only that which Scripture expressly requires may be declared necessary for faith.

Moreover it was Melanchthon, not Luther, who drew up the standard statement of evangelical doctrine. Luther did not dictate forms of public worship or church government or detailed codes of behavior. Points not clearly fixed by Scripture must remain in the realm of freedom. Within this framework, for the sake of good order, church authorities in various regions were to use their best judgment in setting up the forms and standards which should guide the life of the church.

Finally, Luther did not try to dictate decisions or policy in public affairs. Though his advice was frequently sought by rulers and town councils, he knew that a theologian has no superiority in this field. Such questions belong to the public authorities, who should apply to them their best practical judgment and a Christian sense of responsibility for the welfare of the people.

So much for an elementary sampling of Luther's personal qualities. The topic can be pursued almost endlessly. But such a method by itself does not penetrate very deeply into a personality. You cannot understand a man simply in terms of his qualities and temperament. You must also examine the record of his deeds and the results that issued from them.

30. What Did He Do?

In some areas it is fairly easy to measure Luther's achievements; in others, it is much more difficult.

The Writer

The sheer bulk of his literary output is awesome by any standard. During his lifetime over four hundred of his works were published, some very brief, to be sure, but many quite substantial. Few Christian theologians in history match him in productivity. The modern critical edition of Luther's works, not quite finished, runs to more than a hundred large thick volumes. We have over two thousand of his sermons and over three thousand letters, not to mention more than six thousand items of "table talk" collected by guests. Often the reader will wish that Luther had dashed off less and polished more. But he was living on the scene of fast-breaking events, and his judgment was in constant demand. He was living at the crossroads of several radically different conceptions of Christianity, and his insights were eagerly requested. The surprising thing, really, is that so very much of his outpouring remains to this day fresh and thought-provoking and sound. He could polish carefully, too, as we see for example in his masterful *Small Catechism* and in his Bible translation.

Luther's style of writing has exerted as great an influence on the German language as Shakespeare's on English. He could coin sparkling expressions like the English bard, write majestically soaring thoughts like John Milton, spin homely stories and quote proverbs and clothe a profound message in memorable simplicity like Abraham Lincoln.

The range of Luther's writing is impressive. He wrote for simple children and peasants, for burgomasters and princes; with scholars he discussed the subtlest points of theology and tackled the intricate problems of translating and interpreting the Bible. Christian literature in many fields has been lastingly enriched by Luther's pen, and in many realms of Christian thought he is still a potent influence. To find another man who matches Luther's importance as a Bible translator, one would have to turn to Jerome, the learned monk who put the Scriptures into Latin at the dawn of the Middle Ages. English hymnody produced no figure to compare with Luther until Isaac Watts and Charles Wesley. Some of Luther's devotional tracts and sermons rank with the treasures of the ages, and his catechisms stand without a peer in their class. His contribution in liturgies is not so directly noticeable now, but indirectly his attitude and his principles regarding public worship stll retain great importance in evangelical Christendom.

The Preacher

Few men have equalled Luther's power as a preacher. He had a gift of communicating directly with people and of making them sense the enormous importance of God's presence for their lives. In his preaching he did not always live up to his own advice to be brief—as he once put it: "Stand up, speak up, shut up!" But he did try to remember that a sermon is meant to nourish God's people, including the simplest person in the congregation. "A preacher should feed the simple folk milk, for every day the need arises anew to present the fundamentals of the faith. In my sermons I do not think of Bugenhagen, Jonas, and Melanchthon, for they know as much as I do. So I preach not to them but to my little Hans and Lena and Elsa [his niece]."

The Thinker

Luther remains remarkably influential in the realm of theology. This judgment is sometimes disputed. Luther is occasionally portrayed as a man of great heroic action but of little mental power, or even as a fickle weathervane or a blustering windbag in theology. Such an estimate overlooks the way successive generations have found themselves compelled to wrestle with Luther's thought. Even today at the front ranks of theological discussion Luther's opinions are still a force to be contended with. Among theologians who lived before the modern age, probably no others but Augustine, Thomas Aquinas, and Calvin equally deserve to be described in such terms.

Luther's ideas on social, cultural, and educational matters, too, have had a considerable impact in the shaping of Protestantism, and particularly of modern Germany. Here as elsewhere his limitations also are visible. To mention one example, a great modern German historian regards it as Luther's greatest limitation that he educated his people too little in public responsibility. On this point we are moving in a realm where measuring is much more difficult and we should tread cautiously.

Some men claim that Luther won for the modern world its sense of personal liberty, the freedom of the human conscience. Others declare that it was Luther who unleashed the disastrous modern mood of secularism and individualism. The word secularism describes the attitude of men who plan and conduct their lives with no regard for God's authority, as if this world alone counts. Individualism is the attitude of a man who thinks he is a law unto himself and acknowledges no standard beyond himself. Neither attitude applies accurately to Luther. His explicit contribution to modern personal liberties is real but limited. He saw and boldly attacked the tyranny of the church. Far less clearly did he discern how other tyrannies—of dogmatism, for instance—could develop in his reformed church. Still less did he realize that the tyranny of the state might become a worse calamity than that of the medieval church.

It may be argued that, far from promoting secularism and individualism, Luther offers important help in curbing them both. There is truth in the claim that Luther's heroic stand at Worms struck a mighty blow for "the right of private judgment." But Luther by no means taught thereby that every man's conscience is a proper supreme authority, even for himself. The most important thing for him was the foundation on which his conscience stood: "My conscience is captive to the Word of God!" This recognition of a divine authority above himself is Luther's curb of both secularism and individualism. At the same time this recognition is the source of true freedom and spiritual strength, both personal and social. At Worms Luther was declaring not so much "the right of private judgment" as the necessity of personal responsibility.

The Reformer

The deepest, most difficult question of all the questions about Luther's achievements remains. Did he really shatter the church? Did he, as Aleander charged, "rend the seamless robe of Christ"? Your answer will be based chiefly on your understanding of the Christian faith. The counterclaim of Protestants is that Luther broke the papal stranglehold upon the church and upon the proclamation of the gospel. One report by Aleander stated the Lutheran intention with perfect accuracy: "They have convinced themselves that they can be good Christians while opposing the pope, and that the catholic faith [the faith of the universal church] can stand under these conditions." We must keep clearly in mind that "pope" here means the papal system, not the personal character of the bishop of Rome. Even though some popes have led shameful lives, say Roman Catholics, the papacy remains holy, for it is the divinely appointed power to rule the church on earth. No, reply Evangelicals, even though some popes have been personally admirable, the office of the papacy in the Roman Catholic sense is wrong. "Others before me have attacked the pope's life, I have attacked his doctrine," wrote Luther. Consequently, in the Protestant assault, "pope" refers to "the walls of the Romanists" which thwarted a true reform of the church. Luther found that the church under Roman Catholic piloting had drifted far off course. When he tried to bring it back, Rome insisted that it was not off course and expelled him. Evangelicals could not acknowledge that the church of Christ is identical with the Roman Catholic system of guiding it. The sovereign gospel itself sets up the standards for identifying the real church: it is not a sovereign church which sets the standards for identifying the gospel.

We must remember, too, that the rupture in the church during the Reformation was not the first in Christian history. Several centuries earlier virtually all of Eastern Christendom had rejected Rome's pretensions to rule the universal church. The Reformation, therefore, was a split in Western Christendom. This fact does little to soften the tragedy of the Reformation rupture, but it helps to place our present responsibility for the church of Christ in fuller perspective.

In any case, Luther's movement helped to revitalize all of Western Christendom. Even Roman Catholicism, finally shaken out of its complacency by the evangelical challenge, owes some debt to Luther for its own revival.

Luther's personal leadership needs to be emphasized here. Amid the fearful pressures and confusions of his age, he succeeded in keeping the Reformation a basically religious movement. In weaker or less sure hands it might have been captured by visionaries, by social agitators, by nationalists, or by the princes. Luther showed mistakes and weaknesses here and there as a leader, but his labors to keep the gospel sovereign, not a pawn for human progress, were a mighty achievement.

31. What Did He Really Want?

BUT we have not tuned in to the deepest message of Martin Luther. When you try to understand something historical, it is not enough to inquire what took place. You must proceed to ask next, what does it mean? We must listen to what Luther was really trying to say to his own day and to ours as well.

"I have heard that among other follies he teaches that councils have erred; that every layman, if he is in a state of grace, is able to administer the sacrament of the altar; that marriage is dissolvable and fornication is no sin; and that everything takes place according to the law of fate. Besides his errors I learned that he is most imprudent, quite unchaste, and ignorant of the church's doctrine." So a papal ambassador reported in 1521. "You want a great rebellion, not a reform," charged a theologian. "As Luther set out to kill all obedience to the church authorities, he secretly wished to do the same to the civil powers," asserted a dispatch of Aleander. These are a few of the milder charges by his adversaries. Little wonder, with such impressions abroad, that Luther's message has frequently met ostracism, contempt, and distortion even to this day.

Luther's lasting significance, however, is scarcely more recognizable in the judgments of some admirers who set him up as a creative genius or a model saint. It is not Luther's "genius," his uniqueness, which is enduringly important, but that which he shared so helpfully with others—his message of Jesus Christ. It is no article of evangelical belief that Martin Luther was a "saint." He did not urge, as Paul did, "Be imitators of me." On the contrary, he regarded himself as "not worthy of praise." "Men may call me a Lutheran, but they misjudge me; or at best I am a poor and weak Lutheran. May God strengthen me." It was not for his life that he wished to be heard, but for his "doctrine," his message.

Let God Be God

This was a message for anyone who tries to decide what to do and what to be without taking God into account. Luther was aware that God remains God whether we wish it or not; we all live out our lives in his presence whether we acknowledge him or not.

Even more, the gospel was a message for people who seek God, but seek him wrongly. This was a problem which Luther could describe vividly and passionately; it was the fiery trial through which he himself had had to pass. Not only the worst men, but even the "better" ones (in the world's judgment), said Luther in one of his sharpest expressions, make the mistake of refusing to "let God be God." They want to tell God how to take care of them and how to run the world, how to reward the good and punish the wicked.

No! said Luther. First we must listen to what God says about himself and us and the world. God opens his heart to us in Jesus Christ. When Luther stopped making Christ into a stern taskmaster, another lawgiver, and received him instead simply as "the mirror of the Father's heart," his whole relation to God changed. Listening to God, he also understood himself better: "Let God be God, confident that he knows you better than you yourself do." Thereby he could also be realistic about himself and other men. Supremely, in Christ, he could trust that he had become a member of God's own family, kept in God's own care.

Living Faithfully

Accurately, colorfully, and helpfully, by his career and by his teachings, Luther still makes real for us the constant battle a man must wage in order to live his life faithfully in the presence of God. This is an important part of Luther's legacy to Christendom. In one sense our own struggle is different because Luther blazed a trail ahead of us. But in another sense the battle of life remains the same for every man. Luther is helpful because he leads us to the point where each man must take his own part, where each man must walk by himself. Every man must do his own believing, Luther declared, just as one day every man will have to do his own dying. No other man, no organization, no church can believe for him. And regardless of what a man says about his faith, his real faith is the personal conviction and the personal commitment by which he himself lives and dies.

A living Christian faith is never won once and for all; it remains a risk until the day we die because it contradicts the notions men naturally trust in for their security. That is why faith is a perpetual battle. It is a daily conscious commitment to the will of God, choosing God above all alternatives.

Joyful Daring

"This is the nature of faith," said Luther, "that it dares trust in God's grace. It requires a free surrender and joyful daring upon an unfelt, untried, unknown goodness." To be a Christian means to be always becoming a Christian, he insisted.

Yet this very daring brings a man a sure experience of the fatherly goodness of God. "God can make himself known only through those works which he manifests in us, and which we feel and experience within ourselves. But where there is this experience, there a hearty love for him is born, the heart overflows with gladness, and goes leaping and dancing for the great pleasure it has found in God."

The Christian's joy and assurance are deeper than any security based on self-interest. "I would not want my soul to be in my own hands. If it were, the devil would long ago have snatched it away in an instant, as a vulture snatches a chick. But neither the devil nor anyone will tear it from the hand of Christ, to whom I have commended it."

Such a faith not only makes a Christian secure, but it also keeps him "working through love," eager in the service of his fellowmen. As Luther told the unruly Wittenbergers in 1522: "Through love we must do unto one another as God has done unto us through faith. A faith without love is not enough—rather it is not faith at all, but a counterfeit." In a passage on the Christian's responsibility as a citizen, Luther wrote: "Since a true Christian lives and labors on earth not for himself, but for his neighbor, the whole spirit of his life impels him to do even that which he does not have to do, but which is profitable and necessary for his neighbor."

Help for Troubles

The Christian's faith, taught Luther, is one which can stand the blows of suffering. But that is a hard lesson to learn. "It vexes me not a little that I, a doctor, with all my learning, must remain willy-nilly in the same class with my little Hans and Magdalena. Who has ever understood all the meaning of the words, 'Our Father, who art in heaven'? When we trust in these words we know that the God who made heaven and earth is our Father, and that we are his children and none can hurt us. The angel Gabriel is my servant, Raphael is my groom, and all the other angels ministers to my various needs. Then, perhaps, my good Father turns around and has me cast into prison or beheaded or drowned, to test whether I have really learned these words, or even the single word 'Father.' For the faith in our hearts wavers and our weakness suggests a doubt: 'How do I know whether this is true?' The hardest word in all scripture to understand is 'your' in the First Commandment: 'I am the LORD your God.' "

Through and beyond his spiritual "assaults," however, Luther did learn the lesson. One of his favorite stories in the Bible was that of the Canaanite woman who refused to accept an answer of no from Jesus (Matthew 15). Luther applied this story to our own struggles for faith. "All of Christ's answers were more like no than yes. This shows how our heart feels in despondency. It sees nothing but a plain no. Therefore, it must turn to the deep hidden yes under the no, and hold with a firm faith to God's Word." Persistency is an essential dimension of faith.

It has been truly observed, "Only that which passes the test of death can also stand the test of life." Retelling the story of Abraham's willingness to sacrifice Isaac, Luther remarked, "See how God's majesty is at hand in the hour of death. We say, 'In the midst of life we die.' God answers, 'No, in the midst of death we live!' " Luther's own faith faced death sturdily, not only during his days of danger at the beginning of the Reformation, but also when old age came upon him. At his funeral his friend Dr. Jonas painted a vivid picture of the reformer's last days. Many months before he died, Luther had written in his Psalter and prayer book twenty comforting biblical verses, and he pondered them often. For several weeks before his death, he stood daily before the open window of his chamber and prayed aloud. This he did so fervently that his friends were astounded. Finishing his prayer, said Jonas, he would turn again to his friends, "happy as though he had cast off a burden."

It was such a faith that enabled Luther in turn to be so helpful to troubled people. "No one could pray more energetically and earnestly than he, and no one could more genuinely comfort the afflicted," was the tribute of an old friend. The two thoughts indeed belong together.

The Church Is Necessary

"With the church I have in common the teaching of Christ." All that Luther said about the Christian faith has its setting in the church. Faith is never just a private affair. The church is "the mother of every Christian"; in becoming a Christian a man is made a living part of the body of Christ. "Thank God, a seven-year-old child now knows what the church is, namely, holy believers and sheep who hear the voice of their Shepherd," wrote Luther. In spite of all the faults he saw in the church, he loved to describe it as "a holy Christian people," that is, God's own family. He loved to emphasize the fellowship of Christ's followers with their Lord and with one another. His magnificent explanation of the Third Article of the creed in the *Small Catechism* brings the personal and corporate facets of Christianity into a beautiful harmony: "The Holy Spirit has called me through the Gospel, enlightened me with his gifts, and sanctified and kept me in true faith. In the same way he calls, gathers, enlightens, and sanctifies the whole Christian church on earth and keeps it united with Jesus Christ in the one true faith. In this Christian church day after day he fully forgives my sins and the sins of all believers. On the last day he will raise me and all the dead and give me and all believers in Christ eternal life. This is most certainly true."

Christ Our Master

"Christ alone is our master." That phrase is the whole message of this man who sought God—and found him. Not with plans and programs, not with calculating and compromising did Martin Luther earn a name that endures through the ages, but by persistently, persuasively bringing the living name of Jesus Christ to men's hearts. Never did Luther hint that his teaching was right just because he said so or because he had figured it out. Indeed, he went out of his way to assert the opposite. "My teaching is not my own," he said, but Christ's. "Our theology is certain, because it takes us outside ourselves. I do not need to rely upon my conscience, my senses, and my actions, but I rely upon the promise and the truth of God, which never deceive."

Away With Idols

Luther's mission involved him in battles throughout his life. Idols in the Roman Catholic church had to be unmasked and attacked. Roman Catholicism he saw as a sect and not "the church" of Christ. At best, he held, it was a partial representation of the church, and at worst, when it actually contradicted the gospel itself, the Antichrist. Idols among the Protestants who opposed Rome also had to be unmasked and attacked. Anti-Catholicism was not the gospel. Neither were many of the practices which various Protestants substituted for the Roman Catholic system. In addition, idols in "the world" in which and to which the gospel was proclaimed had to be exposed and destroyed.

Luther was well aware of some new idols arising in his own camp, and he did his best to oppose them. He did not so clearly perceive others, as we have mentioned. Yet even in such cases Luther gives us guidance for correcting Luther. As a Christian is never perfected in this life, but is always becoming what he should be, so the reformation of the church is never finished on earth. "The church always in process of being reformed" is Luther's portrait of the people of God in the world. That transformation takes place when everything about the church—its members, its practices, its teachings, its hopes—is brought again and again under the standard which Luther made supreme: "Christ alone is our master."

Lasting Legacy

Martin Luther's lasting legacy to the world is the persistent search of a man for God and the sturdy faith of the man who found him. His was a faith which brought new life and light to Christendom. No longer did Jesus Christ sit frowning on the rainbow. True, he is the God who will come to judge the quick and the dead. But behind this picture, Luther found again the Christ who "for us men and for our salvation came down from heaven," and found in him "the mirror of the Father's heart," the perfect expression of God's "sheer, unutterable love." Christ's promises we can trust. Christ's will we can submit ourselves to obey. With this message Luther does not die, but lives, and proclaims the deeds of the Lord.

A Martin Luther Sampler

The Christian and Christ: Faith

1

*Every man has a god, Luther declares in explaining
the First Commandment.*

What is it to have a god? What is God?

Answer: A god is that to which we look for all good and in which
we find refuge in every time of need. To have a god is nothing else
than to trust and believe him with our whole heart. . . . The trust
and faith of the heart alone make both God and an idol. If your
faith and trust are right, then your God is the true God. On the
other hand, if your trust is false and wrong, then you have not the
true God. For these two belong together, faith and God. That to
which your heart clings and intrusts itself is, I say, really your God.
(1)

2

*Luther had a high opinion of the Ten Command-
ments.*

Here, then, we have the Ten Commandments, a summary of
divine teaching on what we are to do to make our whole life pleasing to God. They are the true fountain from which all good works
must spring, the true channel through which all good works must
flow. (2)

3

What does it mean to fulfill God's law?

God judges according to what is in the depths of the heart. . . .

For even though you keep the law outwardly, with works, from fear of punishment or love of reward, nevertheless you do all this unwillingly . . . with reluctance and under compulsion. For if the law were not there, you would prefer to act otherwise. The conclusion is that from the bottom of your heart you hate the law.

. . . Doing the works of the law and fulfilling the law are two very different things. . . .

To fulfill the law, however, is to do its works with pleasure and love, to live a godly and good life of one's own accord, without the compulsion of the law. This pleasure and love for the law is put into the heart by the Holy Spirit, as St. Paul says in Romans 5[:5]. But the Holy Spirit is not given except in, with, and by faith in Jesus Christ, as St. Paul says in the introduction. Faith, moreover, comes only through God's Word or gospel, which preaches Christ, saying that he is God's Son and a man, and has died and risen again for our sakes, as he says in 3[:25], 4[:25], and 10[:9].

So . . . faith alone makes a person righteous and fulfills the law. (3)

4

What is sin?

Sin, in the Scripture, means not only the outward works of the body but also all the activities that move men to do these works, namely, the inmost heart, with all its powers. . . . The Scriptures look especially into the heart and single out the root and source of all sin, which is unbelief in the inmost heart. (4)

5

Forgiveness of sins, then, is a divine gift, not only canceling my guilt but restoring me to God's favor.

What greater gift could [God] have promised than forgiveness of sins, which is nothing other than grace, peace, life, inheritance, eternal honor and blessedness in God? (5)

When he forgives, he forgives everything completely and leaves nothing unforgiven. When I am free of sin, I am also free of death, devil, and hell; I am a son of God, a lord of heaven and earth. (6)

6

How does faith alone "justify"—make us right with God?

. . . The entire Scripture of God is divided into two parts: commandments and promises. . . . The commandments show us what we ought to do but do not give us the power to do it. They are intended to teach man to know himself, that through them he may recognize his inability to do good and may despair of his own ability. . . .

. . . Here the second part of Scripture comes to our aid, namely, the promises of God . . . , saying, "If you wish to fulfill the law and not covet, as the law demands, come, believe in Christ in whom grace, righteousness, peace, liberty, and all things are promised you. If you believe, you shall have all things. . . ." (7)

7

So the Creed teaches us how we may fulfill the commandments.

The [Ten Commandments] teach us what we ought to do; the Creed tells what God does for us and gives to us. . . . The Ten Commandments do not by themselves make us Christians, for God's wrath and displeasure still remain on us because we cannot fulfill his demands. But the Creed brings pure grace and makes us upright and pleasing to God. Through this knowledge we come to love and delight in all the commandments of God because we see that God gives himself completely to us, with all his gifts and his power, to help us keep the Ten Commandments. . . . (8)

8

Indeed, the Creed, which is the summary of God's revelation in scripture, teaches us what God is like.

Here in the Creed you have the entire essence of God, his will, and his work exquisitely depicted in very short but rich words. . . . Although the whole world has sought painstakingly to learn what God is and what he thinks and does, yet it has never succeeded in the least. But here you have everything in richest measure. In these three articles God himself has revealed and opened to us the most profound depths of his fatherly heart, his sheer, unutterable love. He created us for this very purpose, to redeem and sanctify us. Moreover, having bestowed upon us everything in heaven and on earth, he has given us his Son and his Holy Spirit, through whom he brings us to himself. . . . We could never come to recognize the Father's favor and grace were it not for the Lord Christ, who is a mirror of the Father's heart. Apart from him we see nothing but an angry and terrible Judge. But neither could we know anything of Christ, had it not been revealed by the Holy Spirit. (9)

9

God's love is creative—a sheer miracle.

The love of God does not find but creates the object of its love, whereas the love of man is created by the object of its love.

. . . Thus sinners are lovely because they are loved; they are not loved because they are lovely. That is why human love shuns sinners and evil men. As Christ said, "I came not to call the righteous but sinners" (Matthew 9:13). And that is what love of the cross means. It is a love born of the cross, which betakes itself not to where it can find something good to enjoy, but where it may confer good to the wicked and the needy. (10)

10

Living "in Christ" the Christian becomes a new man.

The third incomparable benefit of faith is that it unites the soul with Christ as a bride is united with her bridegroom. . . .

. . . Christ is God and man in one person. . . . He cannot sin, die, or be condemned; his righteousness, life, and salvation are unconquerable, eternal, omnipotent. By the wedding ring of faith he shares in the sins, death, and pains of hell which are his bride's. As a matter of fact, he makes them his own and acts as if . . . he himself had sinned; he suffered, died, and descended into hell that he might overcome them all. Now since it was such a one who did all this, and death and hell could not swallow him up, these were necessarily swallowed up by him in a mighty duel; for his righteousness is greater than the sins of all men, his life stronger than death, his salvation more invincible than hell. Thus the believing soul by means of the pledge of its faith is free in Christ, its bridegroom, free from all sins, secure against death and hell, and is endowed with the eternal righteousness, life, and salvation of Christ its bridegroom. (11)

11

This announcement of the gift of Christ is the gospel.

. . . Do not make Christ into a Moses. . . . The chief article and foundation of the gospel is that before you take Christ as an example, you accept and recognize him as a gift, as a present that God has given you and that is your own. . . . [Gospel] means a joyful, good, and comforting "message." . . .

Now when you have Christ as the foundation and chief blessing of your salvation, then the other part follows: that you take him as your example, giving yourself in service to your neighbor, just as you see that Christ has given himself for you. . . .

So you see that the gospel is really not a book of laws and commandments which requires deeds of us, but a book of divine promises in which God promises, offers, and gives us all his possessions and benefits in Christ. (12)

12

The good news about Christ is the heart of the Word.

. . . One thing, and only one thing, is necessary for Christian life, righteousness, and freedom. That one thing is the most holy Word of God, the gospel of Christ. . . . The soul can do without anything except the Word of God and . . . where the Word of God is missing there is no help at all for the soul.

. . . "What then is the Word of God, and how shall it be used, since there are so many words of God?" I answer: The . . . Word is the gospel of God concerning his Son, who was made flesh, suffered, rose from the dead, and was glorified through the Spirit who sanctifies. To preach Christ means to feed the soul, make it righteous, set it free, and save it, provided it believes the preaching. Faith alone is the saving and efficacious use of the Word of God. . . .

(13)

13

If faith is a divine gift, it is also a personal decision; it must be your own.

. . . This you must know and confess in your heart that it is true; and if you are not conscious of it, then you have no faith, and the Word only hangs about your ears and swims on your tongue like foam on water. . . . (14)

14

Prayer is the crossroads between having God and needing God.

Mankind is in such a situation that no one can keep the Ten Commandments perfectly, even though he has begun to believe. Besides, the devil, along with the world and our flesh, resists our efforts with all his power. Consequently nothing is so necessary as to call upon God incessantly and drum into his ears our prayer that he may give, preserve, and increase in us faith and obedience to the Ten Commandments and remove all that stands in our way and hinders us from fulfilling them. (15)

. . . When one ponders well [God's] divine works in the depths of his heart and regards them with wonder and gratitude . . . ; when the words, not nicely chosen or prescribed, flow forth in such a way that the spirit comes seething with them, and the words live and have hands and feet, in fact, the whole body and life with all its members strives and strains for utterance—that is indeed a worship of God in spirit and truth, and such words are all fire, light, and life. (16)

15

In temptations and trials, God is our refuge and help.

This, then, is "leading us not into temptation" when God gives us power and strength to resist, even though the tribulation is not removed or ended. For no one can escape temptations and allurements as long as we live in the flesh and have the devil prowling about us. We cannot help but suffer tribulations, and even be entangled in them, but we pray here that we may not fall into them and be overwhelmed by them.

To feel temptation, therefore, is quite a different thing from consenting and yielding to it. We must all feel it, though not all to the same degree; some have more frequent and severe temptations than others. Youths, for example, are tempted chiefly by the flesh; older people are tempted by the world. Others, who are concerned with spiritual matters (that is, strong Christians) are tempted by the devil. But we cannot be harmed by the mere feeling of temptation as long as it is contrary to our will and we would prefer to be rid of it. If we did not feel it, it could not be called a temptation. But to consent to it is to give it free rein and neither resist it nor pray for help against it. (17)

... [God] lets the godly become powerless and to be brought low, until everyone supposes their end is near, whereas in these very things He is present to them with all His power, yet so hidden and in secret that even those who suffer the oppression do not feel it but only believe. There is the fullness of God's power and His outstretched arm. For where man's strength ends, God's strength begins, provided faith is present and waits on Him. And when the oppression comes to an end, it becomes manifest what great strength was hidden underneath the weakness. Even so, Christ was powerless on the cross; and yet He performed His mightiest work and conquered sin, death, world, hell, devil, and all evil. (18)

The Christian and the Means of Grace

16

It is the work of the Holy Spirit to bring Christ to us, and us to Christ.

"I believe that the Holy Spirit makes me holy, as his name implies." How does he do this? . . . "Through the Christian church, the forgiveness of sins, the resurrection of the body, and the life everlasting." In the first place, he has a unique community in the world. It is the mother that begets and bears every Christian through the Word of God. The Holy Spirit reveals and preaches that Word, and by it he illumines and kindles hearts so that they grasp and accept it, cling to it, and persevere in it. (19)

17

What is the church?

I believe that there is on earth a little holy flock or community
of pure saints under one head, Christ. It is called together by the
Holy Spirit in one faith, mind, and understanding. It possesses a
variety of gifts, yet is united in love without sect or schism. Of this
community I also am a part and member, a participant and co-
partner in all the blessings it possesses. I was brought to it by the
Holy Spirit and incorporated into it through the fact that I have
heard and still hear God's Word, which is the first step in entering
it. Before we had advanced this far, we were entirely of the devil,
knowing nothing of God and of Christ. Until the last day the Holy
Spirit remains with the holy community or Christian people.
Through it he gathers us, using it to teach and preach the Word.
By it he creates and increases sanctification, causing it daily to grow
and become strong in the faith and in the fruits of the Spirit.

. . . Everything in the Christian church is so ordered that we may
daily obtain full forgiveness of sins through the Word and through
signs [sacraments] appointed to comfort and revive our consciences
as long as we live. Although we have sin, the Holy Spirit sees to it
that it does not harm us because we are in the Christian church,
where there is full forgiveness of sin. God forgives us, and we forgive, bear with, and aid one another. (20)

18

*This forgiveness is not automatic. It means that
our gracious God, accepting us where we are,
changes us into what he wants us to be.*

Since holiness has begun and is growing daily, we await the time
when our flesh will be put to death, will be buried with all its un-
cleanness, and will come forth gloriously and arise to complete and
perfect holiness in a new, eternal life. Now we are only halfway
pure and holy. The Holy Spirit must continue to work in us
through the Word, daily granting forgiveness until we attain to
that life where there will be no more forgiveness. In that life are
only perfectly pure and holy people, full of goodness and righteousness, completely freed from sin, death, and all evil, living in new,
immortal, and glorified bodies. (21)

19

*Not only does the church call us to life with God,
it also calls men to live together in love, as Luther
says in explaining the Lord's Prayer.*

It is Thy will that we not only call Thee Father, but that all of us together call Thee our Father, and thus offer our prayers with one accord for all: Grant us, therefore, brotherly love and unity, that we may know and think of one another as true brethren and sisters, and pray to Thee, our one common Father, for all men and for every man, even as one child prays for another to its father. (22)

20

*Through baptism all Christians are equally priests
in the church. Ministers are persons assigned to a
special responsibility in it.*

Not only are we the freest of kings, we are also priests forever, which is far more excellent than being kings, for as priests we are worthy to appear before God to pray for others and to teach another divine things. (23)

. . . We are all equally priests, that is to say, we have the same power in respect to the Word and the sacraments. However, no one may make use of this power except by the consent of the community or by the call of a superior. (For what is the common property of all, no individual may arrogate to himself, unless he is called.) (24)

. . . "If all who are in the church are priests, how do these whom we now call priests differ from laymen?" . . . Holy Scripture makes no distinction between them, although it gives the name "ministers," "servants," "stewards" to those who are now proudly called popes, bishops, and lords and who should according to the ministry of the Word serve others and teach them the faith of Christ and the freedom of believers. Although we are all equally priests, we cannot all publicly minister and teach. We ought not to do so even if we could. (25)

What, then, are the priests and bishops? Answer: Their government is not a matter of authority or power, but a service and an office, for they are neither higher nor better than other Christians. Therefore, they should impose no law or decree on others without their will and consent. Their ruling is rather nothing more than the inculcating of God's word, by which they guide Christians and overcome heresy. . . . Christians can be ruled by nothing except God's word, for Christians must be ruled in faith, not with outward works. (26)

21

The church gathers to worship God and present to him its prayers.

. . . [True spiritual worship] is the adoration or bowing of the heart, so that from the bottom of your heart you thereby show and confess yourself to be his subordinate creature. For from this you see that true worship can be nothing else than faith; it is faith's sublimest activity with respect to God. (27)

This common prayer is precious and most powerful, and it is for its sake that we come together. For this reason also the Church is called a House of Prayer, because in it we are as a congregation with one accord to consider our need and the needs of all men, present them before God, and call upon Him for mercy. . . . What sense is there in our coming together into a House of Prayer . . . if we scatter these prayers, and so distribute them that everyone prays only for himself, and no one has any regard for the other, nor concerns himself for another's need? (28)

22

The church also gathers to receive God's Word. This Word is primarily the living and creative Word, Jesus Christ, the head of the church. Because this Word is given to us in the Scriptures, the central purpose of the church's worship is to offer men the biblical Word.

It is not God's Word just because the church speaks it; rather, the church comes into being because God's Word is spoken. The church does not constitute the Word, but is constituted by the Word. (29)

. . . The chief and greatest aim of any Service is to preach and teach God's Word. (30)

Wherever, therefore, you hear or see this Word preached, believed, confessed, and acted on, do not doubt that there must be a true *ecclesia sancta catholica* [holy catholic church], a Christian, holy people, even though it be small in numbers; for God's Word does not go away empty (Isaiah 55:11), . . . If there were no other mark than this one alone, it would still be enough to show that there must

be a Christian church there; for God's Word cannot be present without God's people, and God's people cannot be without God's
Word. . . .

This is the thing that does all miracles, sets everything to rights,
upholds everything, accomplishes everything, does everything. . . .

(31)

23

The Word is offered in two special forms: orally,
through the gospel, and dramatically, through the
two sacraments. Since these are both forms of the
Word which creates faith, they are the primary
"marks" by which we can identify the church. In
these "means of grace" God has directed us to
find him.

The external marks, whereby one can perceive where this Church
is on earth, are baptism, the Sacrament, and the Gospel; and not
Rome, or this place, or that. . . . Neither Rome nor the papal power
is a mark of the Church, for that power cannot make Christians,
as baptism and the Gospel do. . . . (32)

Although [God] is present in all creatures, and I might find
him in stone, in fire, in water, or even in a rope, . . . yet he does
not wish that I seek him there apart from the Word, and cast myself into the fire or the water, or hang myself on the rope. He is
present everywhere, but he does not wish that you grope for him
everywhere. Grope rather where the Word is, and there you will
lay hold of him in the right way. Otherwise you are tempting God
and committing idolatry. (33)

. . . It is one thing if God is present, and another if he is present
for you. He is there for you when he adds his Word and binds
himself, saying, "Here you are to find me." (34)

When I preach [Christ's] death, it is in a public sermon in the
congregation, in which I am addressing myself to no one individu-
ally; whoever grasps it, grasps it. But when I distribute the sacrament, I designate it for the individual who is receiving it. . . . (35)

24

Baptism is our adoption into God's family. As
Mark 16:16 says, "He who believes and is bap-
tized will be saved."

Here you see again how precious and important a thing Baptism
should be regarded as being, for in it we obtain such an inex-

177

pressible treasure. . . . Through the Word Baptism receives the power to become the "washing of regeneration," as St. Paul calls it in Titus 3:5.

. . . True, nothing that is in us [saves] but faith. . . . But . . . faith must have something to believe—something to which it may cling and upon which it may stand. Thus faith clings to the water and believes it to be Baptism in which there is sheer salvation and life, not through the water . . . but through its incorporation with God's Word and ordinance. . . .

My faith does not constitute Baptism but receives it. Baptism does not become invalid even if it is wrongly received or used, for it is bound not to our faith but to the Word. (36)

25

Baptism means a lifelong gift for a lifelong task.

These two parts, being dipped under the water and emerging from it, indicate the power and effect of Baptism, which is simply the slaying of the old Adam and the resurrection of the new man, both of which actions must continue in us our whole life long. Thus a Christian life is nothing else than a daily Baptism, once begun and ever continued. . . . What is the old man? He is what is born in us from Adam, irascible, spiteful, envious, unchaste, greedy, lazy, proud, yes, and unbelieving; he is beset with all vices and by nature has nothing good in him. Now, when we enter Christ's kingdom, this corruption must daily decrease so that the longer we live the more gentle, patient, and meek we become, and the more free from greed, hatred, envy, and pride. . . .

Therefore let everybody regard his Baptism as the daily garment which he is to wear all the time. . . . If we wish to be Christians, we must practice the work that makes us Christians. But if anybody falls away from his Baptism let him return to it. . . . As we have once obtained forgiveness of sins in Baptism, so forgiveness remains day by day as long as we live. . . . (37)

26

The Lord's Supper is a "food for souls," and unites
Christians in the church, the body of Christ.

Christ bids me eat and drink in order that the sacrament may be mine and may be a source of blessing to me as a sure pledge and sign—indeed, as the very gift he has provided for me against my sins, death, and all evils.

. . . The Lord's Supper is given as a daily food and sustenance so that our faith may refresh and strengthen itself and not weaken in the struggle but grow continually stronger. For the new life should be one that continually develops and progresses. Meanwhile it must suffer much opposition. . . . For such times, when our heart feels too sorely pressed, this comfort of the Lord's Supper is given to bring us new strength and refreshment. (38)

The *significance* or effect of this sacrament is fellowship of all the saints. From this it derives its common name *synaxis* [Greek] or *communio* [Latin], that is, fellowship. . . . [To commune] means to take part in this fellowship. Hence it is that Christ and all saints are one spiritual body, just as the inhabitants of a city are one community and body. . . . (39)

27

When should we come to the Lord's Supper?

If you are heavy-laden and feel your weakness, go joyfully to the sacrament and receive refreshment, comfort, and strength. If you wait until you are rid of your burden in order to come to the sacrament purely and worthily, you must stay away from it forever. . . . They alone are unworthy who neither feel their infirmities nor admit to being sinners.

. . ."What shall I do if I cannot feel this need or experience hunger and thirst for the sacrament?" Answer: For persons in such a state of mind . . . [I] suggest that they . . . ask whether they are made of flesh and blood. . . .

If you cannot feel the need, therefore, at least believe the Scriptures. . . . They know your flesh better than you yourself do. (40)

The Christian and His Neighbors

28

If faith is genuine, it breaks out into good works.

O it is a living, busy, active, mighty thing, this faith. It is impossible for it not to be doing good works incessantly. It does not ask whether good works are to be done, but before the question is asked, it has already done them, and is constantly doing them. Whoever does not do such works, however, is an unbeliever. He gropes and looks around for faith and good works, but knows neither what faith is nor what good works are. Yet he talks and talks, with many words, about faith and good works.

Faith is a living, daring confidence in God's grace, so sure and certain that the believer would stake his life on it a thousand times. . . . Without compulsion, a person is ready and glad to do good to everyone, to serve everyone, to suffer everything, out of love and praise to God who has shown him this grace. Thus it is impossible to separate works from faith, quite as impossible to separate heat and light from fire. (41)

29

The Christian does good works, not in order to become good, but because God has made him good.

. . . The person is justified and saved, not by works or laws, but by the Word of God, that is, by the promise of his grace, and by faith, that the glory may remain God's. . . .

From this it is easy to know . . . by what standard all the teachings of men concerning works are to be interpreted. If works are sought after as a means to righteousness, . . . and are done under the false impression that through them one is justified, they are made necessary and freedom and faith are destroyed; and this addition to them makes them no longer good but truly damnable works. . . . We do not, therefore, reject good works; on the contrary, we cherish and teach them as much as possible. (42)

30

The motive of a Christian life is gratitude to God and the joy of following Christ in service to our neighbor.

Man . . . should be guided in all his works by this thought and contemplate this one thing alone, that he may serve and benefit others in all that he does, considering nothing except the need and the advantage of his neighbor. Accordingly the Apostle commands us to work with our hands so that we may give to the needy, although he might have said that we should work to support ourselves . . . [Ephesians 4:28]. This is what makes caring for the body a Christian work, that through its health and comfort we may be able to work, to acquire, and lay by funds with which to aid those who are in need, that in this way the strong member may serve the weaker, and we may be sons of God, each caring for and working for the other, bearing one another's burdens and so fulfilling the law of Christ. This is a truly Christian life. Here faith is truly active through love, that is, it finds expression in works of the freest service, cheerfully and lovingly done, with which a man willingly serves another without hope of reward; and for himself he is satisfied with the fullness and wealth of his faith. (43)

31

Faith and love, then, fulfill the Great Commandment.

We conclude, therefore, that a Christian lives not in himself, but in Christ and in his neighbor. Otherwise he is not a Christian. He lives in Christ through faith, in his neighbor through love. By faith he is caught up beyond himself into God. By love he descends beneath himself into his neighbor. Yet he always remains in God and in his love. . . . (44)

32

Christian faith and love come from God himself;
they are gifts of his Holy Spirit. Luther expressed
this insight in his hymn "We Now Implore God
the Holy Ghost.

We now implore God the Holy Ghost
For the true faith, which we need the most,
That in our last moments He may befriend us
And, as homeward we journey, attend us.
　　Lord, have mercy!

Thou sacred Love, grace on us bestow,
Set our hearts with heavenly fire aglow
That with hearts united we love each other,
Of one mind, in peace with every brother.
　　Lord, have mercy!

Thou highest Comfort in every need,
Grant that neither shame nor death we heed,
That e'en then our courage may never fail us
When the Foe shall accuse and assail us.
　　Lord, have mercy! (45)

33

When we pray for "our daily bread," we are pray-
ing for all the things we need for life in this world.

To put it briefly, this petition includes everything that belongs to our entire life in this world; only for its sake do we need daily bread. Now, our life requires not only food and clothing and other necessities for our body, but also peace and concord in our daily business and in associations of every description with the people among whom we live and move—in short, everything that pertains to the regulation of our domestic and our civil or political affairs. For where these two relations are interfered with and prevented from functioning properly, there the necessities of life are also interfered with, and life itself cannot be maintained for any length of time. Indeed, the greatest need of all is to pray for our civil authorities and the government, for chiefly through them does God provide us our daily bread and all the comforts of this life. Although we have received from God all good things in abundance, we cannot retain any of them or enjoy them in security and happiness unless he gives us a stable, peaceful government. For where dissension, strife, and war prevail, there our daily bread is taken away, or at least reduced. (46)

34

The Fourth Commandment*, "Honor your father and your mother," indicates that the family is the basic unit in society.

To fatherhood and motherhood God has given the special distinction, above all estates that are beneath it, that he commands us not simply to love our parents but also to honor them. . . . Thus he distinguishes father and mother above all other persons on earth, and places them next to himself. For it is a much greater thing to honor than to love. . . .

Young people must therefore be taught to revere their parents as God's representatives, and to remember that, however lowly, poor, feeble, and eccentric they may be, they are their own father and mother, given them by God. They are not to be deprived of their honor because of their ways or their failings. Therefore, we are not to think of their persons, whatever they are, but of the will of God, who has created and ordained them to be our parents. In other respects, indeed, we are all equal in the sight of God, but among ourselves there must be this sort of inequality and proper distinctions. (47)

35

The Fourth Commandment is thus the basis of all authority in human relations.

. . . There is more to be said about the various kinds of obedience due to our superiors, persons whose duty it is to command and to govern. Out of the authority of parents all other authority is derived and developed. Where a father is unable by himself to bring up his child, he calls upon a schoolmaster to teach him; if he is too weak, he enlists the help of his friends and neighbors; if he passes away, he confers and delegates his authority and responsibility to others appointed for the purpose. Likewise he must have domestics . . . under him to manage the household. Thus all who are called masters stand in the place of parents and derive from them their power and authority to govern. In the Scriptures they

---

* This is called the Fifth Commandment in the Reformed tradition. Luther kept the arrangement common in the medieval church. The Reformed made two commandments out of the first, and combined into one the prohibitions against coveting.

are all called fathers because in their responsibility they act in the capacity of fathers and ought to have fatherly hearts toward their people.

Thus we have three kinds of fathers presented in this commandment: fathers by blood, fathers of a household, and fathers of the nation. Besides these, there are also spiritual fathers . . . those who govern and guide us by the Word of God. (48)

36

The role of parent carries with it not only authority, but also responsibility.

In addition, it would be well to preach to parents on the nature of their office, how they should treat those committed to their authority. . . . Parents should consider that they owe obedience to God, and that, above all, they should earnestly and faithfully discharge the duties of their office, not only to provide for the material support of their children, servants, subjects, etc., but especially to bring them up to the praise and honor of God. Therefore do not imagine that the parental office is a matter of your pleasure and whim. It is a strict commandment and injunction of God, who holds you accountable for it. (49)

37

The three basic units of human society are the family, the state, and the church. These are the "orders" established by God. In them Christian love is to be practiced.

But the holy orders . . . established by God are these three: the office of priest, the estate of marriage, the civil government. All who are engaged in the clerical office or ministry of the Word are in a holy, proper, good, and God-pleasing order and estate, such as those who preach, administer sacraments, supervise the common chest, sextons and messengers or servants who serve such persons. These are engaged in works which are altogether holy in God's sight.

Again, all fathers and mothers who regulate their household wisely and bring up their children to the service of God are engaged in pure holiness, in a holy work and a holy order. Similarly, when children and servants show obedience to their elders and masters, here too is pure holiness, and whoever is thus engaged is a living saint on earth.

Moreover, princes and lords, judges, civil officers, state officials, notaries, male and female servants and all who serve such persons, and further, all their obedient subjects—all are engaged in pure holiness and leading a holy life before God. . . .

Above these three institutions and orders is the common order of Christian love, in which one serves not only the three orders, but also serves every needy person in general with all kinds of benevolent deeds, such as feeding the hungry, giving drink to the thirsty, forgiving enemies, praying for all men on earth, suffering all kinds of evil on earth, etc. Behold, all of these are called good and holy works. However, none of these orders is a means of salvation. There remains only one way above them all, namely, faith in Jesus Christ. (50)

38
The state bears responsibility for public order and public welfare.

[Worldly government] is a glorious ordinance of God and splendid gift of God, Who has established and instituted it. . . . If there were no worldly government, no man could live because of other men; one would devour the other. . . . It is the function and the honor of worldly government to make men out of wild beasts and to prevent men from becoming wild beasts. . . .

. . . Without government this life cannot continue. Therefore. . . [God] will have it maintained, as is clearly stated in Romans 13 by Paul, and in 1 Peter 2, where it is said that [rulers] are to protect the good and punish the bad. Now who will maintain it except us men, to whom God has committed it and who verily need it for ourselves? . . .

. . . Briefly, then, it is not the law of the fist, but the law of the head that must rule; not force, but wisdom or reason, among the wicked as among the good. (51)

. . . A prince's duty is fourfold: First, toward God there must be true confidence and earnest prayer; second, toward his subjects there must be love and Christian service; third, with respect to his counselors and officials he must maintain an untrammeled reason and unfettered judgment; fourth, with respect to evildoers he must manifest a restrained severity and firmness. Then the prince's job will be done right, both outwardly and inwardly; it will be pleasing to God and to the people. But he will have to expect much envy and sorrow on account of it; the cross will soon rest on the shoulders of such a prince. (52)

. . . A prince leads a multitude with him . . . considering their need and advantage more than his will and pleasure. For when a prince rules after his own mad will and follows his own opinion, he is like a mad driver, who rushes straight ahead with horse and wagon, through bushes, thorns, ditches, water, up hill and down dale, regardless of roads and bridges; he will not drive long; all will go to smash. (53)

39

God stations each person in one "calling" or another in order to serve the common good. Honest work therefore is dignified by God.

At the same time [God] confirms all crafts, classes, and trades . . . , insofar as they are honest and praiseworthy according to their own law. They may be citizens, farmers, shoemakers, tailors, clerks, knights, masters, servants, etc.; for without such . . . no city or country could exist. . . . Such occupations are not contrary to God; and if one wants to serve God, one should not turn up one's nose at them and creep away into a monastery or set up some other sect. Yes, these are all estates established by God to serve Him according to the words of Genesis 3:19: "In the sweat of your face you shall eat bread." (54)

How is it possible that you are not called? You have always been in some state or station; you have always been a husband or wife, or son or daughter, servant or maid. Take even the humblest calling. If you are a husband, do you think you have not enough to do in that calling, to govern your wife, children, servants, and property, so that all may be obedient to God, and that you do no one any wrong? If you are a son or daughter, do you think you have not enough work to keep yourself chaste, pure, and temperate during your youth, obey your parents, and offend no one by word or deed? Again, if you are a servant or a maid, do you think you would go idle if you were to serve your master or mistress with all faithfulness as your calling requires, and also keep your youth under control? Are you a prince, a lord? Who has more to do than you, in order that your subjects may do right, peace may be preserved, and no one may suffer wrong? (55)

. . . These works have been commanded by God, and for this reason they are truly divine works, whether you are a pupil and learn letters, a maid and sweep the house with brooms, or a servant and tend horses or do other things. A monk, of course, leads a more burdensome life and wears more sordid garments; but that he serves God—this he will nevermore be able to say truthfully as can those who serve the household, the state, or the church. (56)

Christ does not ask whether you are a man or a woman, an emperor or a stableman, a mayor or a messenger. He takes all this as it is, and says simply: man shall obey God in his station, and not shy away from it. If you remain in the position which God has assigned you, you can serve God—the man as a man, the woman as a woman, the emperor as an emperor, the citizen as a citizen, each one learning how to acknowledge God and thus glorifying him. (57)

Prayers

40

O Lord God, heavenly Father, pour out, we beseech thee, thy Holy Spirit upon thy faithful people, keep them steadfast in thy grace and truth, protect and comfort them in all temptation, defend them against all enemies of thy Word, and bestow upon Christ's Church militant thy saving peace; through the same thy Son, Jesus Christ our Lord, who liveth and reigneth with thee and the Holy Ghost, one God, world without end. Amen. (58)

41

O our God, we are sorely in need of a shepherd to come and seek us. Therefore we rely completely on the gospel. O Lord, we know that thou dost recognize thine own. May we cling to the assurance that thou are the shepherd who seeks us, thy straying sheep. Save us, O God, for the sake of thine only-begotten Son. Amen. (59)

42

Almighty God, who knowest us to be set in the midst of so many and great dangers, that by reason of the frailty of our nature we cannot always stand upright: Grant us such strength and protection, as may support us in all dangers, and carry us through all temptations; through Jesus Christ, thy Son, our Lord. Amen. (60)

43

O Father, grant us grace and help us to let thy divine will be done in us. Even if it is painful to us, do thou continue to chastise, sting, strike, and burn, and do whatever thou wilt, that thy will alone and not ours may be done. Restrain us, dear Father, and let us not undertake or complete anything according to our own desire and purpose. For our will is opposed to thine. Thy will alone is good, although it does not appear so; and ours is evil, although it may seem good. Amen. (61)

44

Behold, Lord, an empty vessel that needs to be filled. My lord, fill it. I am weak in faith; strengthen thou me. I am cold in love; warm me and make me fervent, that my love may go out to my neighbor. Strengthen my faith and trust in thee. I am poor; thou art rich, and didst come to be merciful to the poor. I am a sinner; thou art upright. With me there is an abundance of sin; in thee is the fullness of righteousness. Therefore, I will remain with thee, from whom I can receive, but to whom I can give nothing. Amen. (62)

45

Grant that neither wrath nor any other bitterness may set up its kingdom within us, but that there may rule within us, by Thy grace, sweet simplicity and brotherly fidelity, and all kindliness, charity and gentleness. Help us to have within us no undue sorrow or sadness, but let joy and gladness in Thy grace and mercy come to us. And help us, finally, that all sin may be turned away from us, so that we may be filled with Thy grace, and with all virtues and good works, and thus become Thy kingdom, so that all our heart, mind and spirit, with all our powers of body and soul, may obediently serve Thee, keep Thy commandments and do Thy will, be ruled by Thee alone, and may not follow after self or flesh or world or devil.

Grant that this Thy kingdom, now begun in us, may increase, and daily grow in power; that indifference to God's service—that subtle wickedness—may not overcome us and make us fall away; but give us rather the power and earnest purpose not only to make a beginning in righteousness, but boldly to go on unto perfection. . . .

Help us that we may remain constant, and that Thy future kingdom may finish and complete this Thy kingdom which is here begun. Amen. (63)

46

Almighty God, heavenly Father, thou Creator of heaven and earth, we are unworthy to ask anything of thee, yet we are moved by thy great mercy and our own needs to pray to thee without ceasing. We are comforted also by thine almighty goodness, from which no gift is too great for thee to give; for thee it is never too difficult or too much to show mercy to all believers. Therefore, O almighty Creator, eternal, merciful God, Heavenly Father, draw us to thyself and grant us to know thy dear Son Jesus Christ, our Savior, in the Holy Spirit and in true and heartfelt faith, through which we have eternal life in the same thy Son, Jesus Christ our Lord. Amen. (64)

47

Come, Holy Spirit, thou one true Comfort of all the distressed, thou Giver of holiness and life, true Teacher of divine truth, O thou wonder and joy of all faithful souls, fill the hearts of thy believers with heavenly comfort. Kindle in us the fire of thy love, that by it all evil desires and the wilfulness of our flesh may be consumed. Pour out upon us poor, unworthy men the rich gifts of divine grace, through which we know Jesus Christ, our Lord and God, and his redemption, and through which we begin in Christ a new and upright life. Grant us to grow daily in these gifts and to remain steadfast to the end, that, guarded from all error through the knowledge of Christ we may increase in all wisdom, and for his sake be led and guided by thee more and more to the praise of God, through the same our Lord Jesus Christ. Amen. (65)

48

O Lord, almighty God, who art love, and who dwellest in love, we poor needy men pray this day that through the Holy Spirit thou wouldst pour into our hearts an unfeigned Christian love, through which we truly love one another not only in words but also in deeds. So may we abundantly prove our faith, as those who have been born from above through the Word of the living God. So guard us that we may not act, under the semblance and name of love, against faith and against thy divine truth, and thus in the end utterly fall away from the true love, which was won for us through the cross and the blood of Christ; through the same our Lord Jesus Christ. Amen. (66)

49

O Heavenly Father, grant us thy grace, that the life, words, deeds, and sufferings of Christ may be preached, known and kept among us in all the world. Grant thy grace that all preachers may proclaim thy Word wholesomely and blessedly throughout the world, and that all who hear thy Word preached may learn to know Christ and sincerely amend their lives. Grant that all preachers may administer the holy sacrament worthily and blessedly, for the good of all Christendom, and that we and all Christians may receive the holy sacrament blessedly and with grace. Amen. (67)

References for the Luther Sampler

1. *Large Catechism**, Ten Commandments, 1–3.
2. *Large Catechism,* Ten Commandments, 311.
3. "Preface to Romans," 1522, *LW* 35, 366, 367–8.
4. "Preface to Romans," *LW* 35, 369.
5. "The Misuse of the Mass," 1521, *LW* 36, 176.
6. "The Sacrament," 1526, *LW* 36, 349–50.
7. "Freedom of a Christian," 1520, *LW* 31, 348–9.
8. *Large Catechism,* Creed, 67–9.
9. *Large Catechism,* Creed, 63–5.
10. "The Heidelberg Disputation," 1518, Thesis 28, *LCC* 16, 295.
11. "Freedom of a Christian," *LW* 31, 351–2.
12. "Brief Instruction on What to Look for and Expect in the Gospels," 1521, *LW* 35, 119–20.
13. "Freedom of a Christian," *LW* 31, 345–6.
14. "Sermon of 1522," *Le* 13, 239.
15. *Large Catechism,* Lord's Prayer, 2.
16. "The Magnificat," 1521, *LW* 21, 326.
17. *Large Catechism,* Lord's Prayer, 106–8.
18. "The Magnificat," *LW* 21, 340.
19. *Large Catechism,* Creed, 40–2.
20. *Large Catechism,* Creed, 51–3, 55.
21. *Large Catechism,* Creed, 57–8.
22. "Brief Explanation of the Lord's Prayer," 1520, *PE* 2, 375.
23. "Freedom of a Christian," *LW* 31, 355.
24. "Babylonian Captivity," 1520, *LW* 36, 116.
25. "Freedom of a Christian," *LW* 31, 356.
26. "Civil Authority," 1523, *LW* 45, 117.
27. "Adoration of the Sacrament," 1523, *LW* 36, 293.
28. "Treatise on Good Works," 1520, *PE* 1, 233–4.
29. "The Misuse of the Mass," 1521, *LW* 36, 144–145.
30. "German Mass," 1526, *PE* 6, 176.
31. "Councils and Church," 1539, *PE* 5, 271.
32. "Papacy at Rome," 1520, *PE* 1, 361.
33. "The Sacrament," *LW* 36, 342.
34. "This Is My Body," 1527, *LW* 37, 68.
35. "The Sacrament," *LW* 36, 348.
36. *Large Catechism,* Baptism, 26–27, 28–29, 53.
37. *Large Catechism,* Baptism, 65–67, 84–86.
38. *Large Catechism,* Lord's Supper, 22, 24–7.
39. "The Blessed Sacrament," 1519, *LW* 35, 50–1.

* Quotations from the *Large Catechism* (translated by Robert H. Fischer) can be found in *The Book of Concord,* Theodore G. Tappert (ed.), (Philadelphia: Muhlenberg Press, 1959).

40. *Large Catechism,* Lord's Supper, 72–4, 75–6.
41. "Preface to Romans," *LW* 35, 370–1.
42. "Freedom of a Christian," *LW* 31, 362–363.
43. "Freedom of a Christian," *LW* 31, 365.
44. "Freedom of a Christian," *LW* 31, 371.
45. *Lutheran Hymnal,* No. 231.
46. *Large Catechism,* Lord's Prayer, 73–4.
47. *Large Catechism,* Ten Commandments, 105, 108.
48. *Large Catechism,* Ten Commandments, 141–2, 158.
49. *Large Catechism,* Ten Commandments, 167–9.
50. "Confession Concerning Christ's Supper," 1528, *LW* 37, 364–5.
51. "On Keeping Children in School," 1530, *PE* 4, 158–60.
52. "Civil Authority," *LW* 45, 126.
53. "Good Works," *PE* 1, 265.
54. "Explanation of Psalm 117," 1530, *LW* 14, 15.
55. "Sermon of 1522," *Le* 10, 242.
56. "Lectures on Genesis," 1535–45, *LW* 3, 218.
57. "Sermon of 1544," *WA* 52, 62–3.
58. Collect for the Festival of the Reformation, *SBH,* p. 113.
59. *Little Book of Prayers,* 1522.
60. A prayer which Luther used in his Latin Litany, *SBH,* p. 161.
61. *A Short Exposition of the Lord's Prayer,* 1519.
62. *Little Book of Prayers.*
63. "A Brief Explanation of the Lord's Prayer," 1520, *PE* 2, 377–378.
64. *Little Book of Prayers.*
65. *Little Book of Prayers* (abridged).
66. *Little Book of Prayers* (abridged).
67. *Little Book of Prayers.*

KEY TO ABBREVIATIONS

Le— *The Precious and Sacred Writings of Martin Luther,* edited by John N. Lenker (Minneapolis, 1904–1909).

LCC—*The Library of Christian Classics,* John Baillie, John T. McNeill, and Henry P. van Dusen, general editors (Philadelphia, 1953–   ).

LW— American edition of *Luther's Works,* edited by Helmut T. Lehmann and Jaroslav Pelikan (Philadelphia and St. Louis, 1955–   ).

PE— *Works of Martin Luther* (Philadelphia, 1915–1943).

WA— *D. Martin Luthers Werke,* Kritische Gesamtausgabe (Weimar, 1883–   ).